BETWEEN ATHENS AND BERLIN

David H. Kelsey

BETWEEN
ATHENS
AND
BERLIN

The Theological
Education
Debate

WILLIAM B. EERDMANS PUBLISHING COMPANY
GRAND RAPIDS, MICHIGAN

Copyright © 1993 by Wm. B. Eerdmans Publishing Co.
255 Jefferson Ave. S.E., Grand Rapids, Mich. 49503
All rights reserved

Printed in the United States of America

ISBN 0-8028-0672-4

Contents

Acknowledgments vii

1. Between "Athens" and "Berlin" 1

2. "Athens" in the Mid-Nineteenth Century 29

3. "Berlin" in Early Twentieth-Century America 49

4. "Athens": Unity and Pluralism
   in the Current Discussion 95

5. "Berlin": Unity and Pluralism
   in the Current Discussion 155

6. "Athens" and "Berlin" in a New Key? 199

Epilogue: Morals of the Tale 221

Index 231

v

Acknowledgments

My own interest in the debate discussed here grew out of several years' involvement in the work of the Association of Theological Schools' Issues Research Committee, chaired at the time by Clark Gilpin and Joseph Hough. Discussions by the Committee of the texts examined here, several of which were written by members of the Committee, helped to focus the issues for me. Leon Pacala, then Executive Director of ATS, invited me to take part in the Committee's work. Robert Wood Lynn, then Senior Vice President for Religion at the Eli Lilly Endowment, encouraged me to undertake the writing and supported the endeavor. Barbara Wheeler offered invaluable editorial and critical advice based on painstaking reading of two drafts. Joseph Mangina skillfully rendered my chaotic corrected drafts into readable text. I am deeply grateful for their excellent company in this project, and for their various and indispensable kinds of help I gladly thank them.

My writing project that grew out of these years of involvement in the work of the Issues Research Committee produced a sibling to this book, *To Understand God Truly: What's Theological about a Theological School* (Louisville: Westminster / John Knox, 1992). They are close to being non-identical twins, having been formed in the same gestation period. The difference between them is this: If, having read the present book's introduction to the debate about theological education and its analysis of the literature produced by the debate, you wonder how I would myself conceive theological education, turn to the other book; if, having read the latter's proposal about how best to analyze and reconceive a theological school, you wonder how I understand other authors with whom I have been in largely implicit conversation, take up this book.

I

Between Athens and Berlin

In the 1980s Christian theological educators in North America
produced the most extensive debate in print about theological
schooling that has ever been published. The debate is remarkable
in several respects. For one thing, it is remarkable that it happened
at all. Most types of higher education in America, from liberal
arts colleges through research universities to schools of medicine
and law, have periodically gone through seasons of self-critical
debate about the nature and purpose of their enterprises. Often
debate has led to educational reform. Such critical self-examination has not, however, been a notable preoccupation of theological
educators. Almost thirty years had passed since the last major,
comprehensive, and theologically self-conscious study of Protestant theological education.[1] It is also remarkable, indeed unprec-

---

1. H. Richard Niebuhr, *The Purpose of the Church and Its Ministry* (New
York: Harper & Row, 1956); H. Richard Niebuhr, Daniel Day Williams, and
James M. Gustafson, *The Advancement of Theological Education* (New York: Harper
& Row, 1957).

edented, that such a sustained debate emerged, not in response to one large study of theological education, but as a conversation among several quite different theological points of view.

Most striking of all, perhaps, is the fact that it has been a *theological* debate. Its central focus has been the question, "What is theological about theological education?" The debate has not focused on pedagogical questions, on variations of the question, "What is the most effective way to teach in theological education?" Presumably, pedagogical insights are applicable to teaching anything. No doubt theological teaching would profit enormously by being more deeply shaped by such insight. But that type of improvement would not necessarily make the education better *theological* education. Nor has the debate focused on questions about the future integrity of the enterprise of theological education: for example, "How can we strengthen and preserve its financial resources?" or "How do we attract abler students?" or "How do we make our course of study more responsive to the churches' multiple demands without fracturing into a collection of unrelated programs?" Rather, the central question in the recent debate has been this: "What is the nature and purpose of specifically *theological* education? What sets it off from other apparently closely related academic enterprises as, precisely, *theological* education?"

The participants in the discussion have largely, although not entirely, been white male faculty members of theological schools that can fairly be described as "mainline Protestant" schools. It is important to acknowledge at the outset that this is a major limitation of the discussion. Theological educators who are women and people of color, Roman Catholic and evangelical Protestant have participated in the discussion. However, with one exception (the feminist Mud Flower Collective's *God's Fierce Whimsy*, discussed in Chapter 4), book-length essays about the the nature and purpose of theological education written from any of their perspectives have not yet been published. Hopefully, that situation will soon be changed.

The premise of this book is that in the meantime it is important for the literature that has been generated by this debate to be widely understood and critically analyzed. This literature is important in fairly obvious ways for theological educators; after all, it is their enterprise that is under scrutiny! It is, I think, also important more broadly for anyone concerned about the health of the enterprise of "doing theology." There are two interlocking reasons why this is the case. The reasons are, first, that the literature reveals deep incoherences in the way theological education is, in actual practice, theologically conceived; and, second, that the literature sharply focuses much of what is at stake in different understandings of "the nature of theology." These two reasons interlock because of a crucial fact in the sociology of theology: the institutional context in which most "intellectually serious" or "formal" theology has been done in North America for more than a century and a half has increasingly been the theological school. Indeed, much of the time the term *theology* is used as shorthand for "academic theology," theology done in the academy and in large part answerable to the academy. Accordingly, if you profoundly reconceive theological schooling, you end up reconceiving what it is to do theology, and vice versa. Clearly, then, it is important for anyone concerned about the health of theological education, or, more broadly, for anyone concerned about the health of theology, to be aware, not simply of one or another of the voices in the debate, but of the overall structure and movement of the debate as a whole. On the one hand, it is important critically to see the force of claims about deep *theological* incoherence in theological education and their implied criticisms of what "theology" has become; on the other hand, it is equally important to see how differing pictures of the nature and purpose of theology call for

3

differing changes in our understanding of the nature and purpose of theological education.

My goals in this book, then, are to give as fair and readable an account as I can of this literature, to describe the debate's internal movement and structure, and to draw attention to what is at stake theologically between contrasting voices in the debate, including what is at stake regarding the nature of theology itself. I identify five voices in this debate that I take to be the most completely developed and importantly contrasting "positions" in the conversation: Edward Farley's *Theologia: The Fragmentation and Unity of Theological Education* and his *The Fragility of Knowledge: Theological Education in the Church and the University;*[2] the Mud Flower Collective's *God's Fierce Whimsy;*[3] Joseph C. Hough, Jr., and John B. Cobb, Jr.'s *Christian Identity and Theological Education;*[4] Max L. Stackhouse's *Apologia: Contextualization, Globalization, and Mission in Theological Education;*[5] and Charles M. Wood's *Vision and Discernment.*[6] Although each of these voices makes important claims in its own right, which I hope to summarize as briefly as clarity and fairness permit, what is most important, I think, is the largely implicit interplay among them of contrasting insights and themes. This is what I mean by "the debate's internal movement and structure." Hence, even more important than summarizing accurately *what* they propose will be the effort to trace the *movement* of their thought as they seek to persuade us of the wisdom of their proposals; so too, more

2. Farley, *Theologia: The Fragmentation and Unity of Theological Education* (Philadelphia: Fortress Press, 1983); *The Fragility of Knowledge: Theological Education in the Church and the University* (Philadelphia: Fortress Press, 1988).

3. *God's Fierce Whimsy* (New York: Pilgrim Press, 1985).

4. Hough and Cobb, *Christian Identity and Theological Education* (Chico: Scholars Press, 1985).

5. Stackhouse, *Apologia: Contextualization, Globalization, and Mission in Theological Education* (Grand Rapids: William B. Eerdmans, 1988).

6. Wood, *Vision and Discernment* (Atlanta: Scholars Press, 1985).

important even than identifying where their proposals explicitly or implicitly *exclude* one another will be the effort to see how tensions among their contrasting but equally valid insights actually *bind them together* and force us to find new conceptualities, new frames-of-reference for our analyses of what is theological about theological education. What I want to throw light on is not simply the important contributions these five voices make one by one but rather what we might call the "field" of conceptual tensions — conceptual conflicts, but also something like conceptual synergisms generated by the debate.

As a kind of axis or armature around which to organize discussion of these voices, I propose a typology. I suggest that for historical reasons Christian theological education in North America is inescapably committed to two contrasting and finally irreconcilable types or models of what education at its best ought to be. They are normative models, models of "excellent" education. For one type I shall suggest that "Athens" be the symbol, for the other "Berlin."[7]

Although persuasive theological arguments can be given for adopting each of these types, neither of them can be said to be somehow theologically mandated by the very nature of Christianity. Indeed, Tertullian's ancient question, "What has Jerusalem to do with Athens?" might suggest that, with its roots in "Jerusalem," Christianity in fact theologically mandates a third type of excellent schooling altogether, one hitherto ignored by major Christian communities. Whatever the theologically normative case might be, however, it is the case de facto that modern North American Christian theological education is committed to "Athens" and "Berlin," and it is committed to both of them for

7. I have developed this typology in greater detail in *To Understand God Truly: What's Theological about a Theological School* (Louisville: Westminster/John Knox, 1992), chaps. 2 and 3.

historical reasons. Moreover, it is deeply committed. Both types of excellent schooling are deeply institutionalized in the practices that constitute American theological education of all sorts; neither one can simply be abandoned by a faculty vote!

Each type of excellent education has definite implications regarding a number of features of theological education, such as the relation between teachers and students, the characteristics looked for in an excellent teacher, what the education aims to do for the student, what the movement of the course of study should be, and the sort of community the school should be. We will return to these implications later in the chapter when we contrast "Athens" and "Berlin" to each other.

Christian theological education in North America is ineluctably located *between* "Athens" and "Berlin." Every theological course of study rests on some sort of more or less implicit negotiated truce between these two models of excellent schooling. My larger point will be that the five major voices in the current debate about theological education represent a set of overlapping, sometimes mutually conflicting, but sometimes mutually deepening and enriching patterns of negotiation between "Athens" and "Berlin." The rest of this chapter is devoted to outlining each "type" and suggesting how theological education came to be assimilated to it.

"Athens"

Because it was the picture of schooling celebrated in the culture of ancient Greece, we will let "Athens" stand for a type of schooling for which paideia is the heart of education. In Greek *paideia* meant a process of "culturing" the soul, schooling as "character formation." It is the oldest picture of education to be found in Christianity and has been powerfully retrieved in the current debate about theological education. By the end of the first century, Christians in a Hellenistic culture had already unselfconsciously come to think of Christianity as a kind of paideia. This model exercised a very long hegemony over Christian understandings of both Christianity and education. Toward the end of *Early Christianity and Greek Paideia,* Werner Jaeger, the foremost historian of paideia, claims that this model of education "can be pursued through the Middle Ages; and from the Renaissance the line leads straight back to the Christian humanism of the fathers of the fourth century A.D."[8] At this end of the historical line, this model was introjected into the debate about theological education by the book that can fairly be said to have started the current discussion, Edward Farley's *Theologia,* "which," in its own words, "purports to promote a Christian *paideia.*"[9]

Of course, the idea of paideia has passed through some important changes during this long history. It was already more than four centuries old when the Christians arrived on the scene. In ancient Athens, "paideia" simply named an unself-conscious educational process through which young free males were "formed" by those virtues they would need in order to function as responsible adult citizens. The process involved the whole person. Their bodies were subjected to physical discipline, and their souls were in-formed by ancient Greece's traditions and customs, chiefly by studying Homer, so that the young would emerge deeply shaped by the dispositions that make for good citizens. The goal of education as paideia was something both very public and very political: the cultivating of politically skilled citizens for an idealized "democratic" self-governing *polis* or city.

By the fourth century B.C., Athenian culture had become

8. Jaeger, *Early Christianity and Greek Paideia* (Cambridge: Harvard University Press, 1961), p. 100.
9. Farley, *Theologia,* p. xi.

7

self-conscious about its ideal of both culture and education — or, more exactly, about education as "culturing" the young.[10] At that point Plato introduced the first major modification in the idea (though, as it turned out, not the practice) of paideia. In the *Republic* he proposed to refine the kind of education needed to provide public leadership by distinguishing two specific forms of paideia. The education of one group, whom Plato called the "Guardians," should aim at inculcating in them the civic traditions and the virtues (chiefly courage) they would need to protect the *polis*. This form of paideia would consist in largely unreflective, mostly rote training in traditional customs and practices. Another group, whom Plato called the "Philosopher Kings," were needed to rule the *polis* wisely and well. To do that they had to be capacitated for knowledge of the Good itself, and not simply for knowledge of traditional beliefs and practices. This would be accomplished by means of a form of paideia that would cultivate in them the "philosophical virtues," shaping in them habits of analytical and critical thinking. Clearly, even in Plato's proposed revision, paideia is a model of excellent education defined by the goal of capacitating people for political and public *action*.

By this point in its career, paideia had come to have four aspects that continue to mark it thereafter, despite changes in other respects.[11] These aspects are largely the legacy of Plato's proposed reform of Athens' traditional educational practices. They became intellectual and cultural commonplaces, generally accepted characteristics of what education "ought" to be, no matter how it was actually conducted. We will abstract them as an ahistorical construct, a type of excellent education, for which "Athens" will be the emblem:

10. Cf. Werner Jaeger, *Paideia*, 3 vols., trans. Gilbert Highet (Oxford: Basil Blackwell, 1939-63), 2:5.

11. See Jaeger, *Paideia*, vol. 2, chaps. 4 and 5.

(1) The goal of paideia, which is the cultivation of the excellence or *arete* of the soul, consists not in acquiring a clutch of virtues but in knowledge of the Good itself. Education as paideia is defined as inquiry into a single, underlying principle of all virtues, their essence. To be shaped by *arete* simply *is* to know the Good.

(2) The Good is not only the underlying essence of the moral and intellectual virtues; it is the highest principle of the universe. It is the divine. Plato came to be understood as the founder of a religion, and paideia was understood to be an education whose goal was in some way religious as well as moral.

(3) The goal of paideia cannot be taught directly — for example, by simply conveying information about various philosophers' doctrines regarding virtue. Knowledge of the Good only comes through contemplation, the ultimate fruit of which is an intuitive insight, a *gnosis* of the Good. Accordingly, all a teacher can provide a student is indirect assistance, intellectual and moral disciplines that will capacitate the student for the student's own moment of insight. This can be accomplished by the study of texts — not merely Homer now, but the philosophers as well, especially Plato.

(4) Insightful knowledge of the Good requires a conversion, a turning around of the soul from preoccupation with appearances to focus on reality, on the Good. This conversion results from a long educational process that Jaeger characterizes as "slow vegetable growth."[12] It requires, like vegetable growth, a climate and nutrients that can only be provided by a society and its culture, by the right *polis*. Education as paideia is inherently communal and not solitary.

Reconceived by Plato, paideia subsequently went through a second major change before Christians appropriated it (or before

12. Jaeger, *Paideia*, 2:228.

it appropriated the Christians). Over centuries, the goal of paideia increasingly shifted from the public to the private realm, from capacitating persons for public and political action to preparing them for inward and religious transformation. Moreover, increasingly it was stressed that divine assistance is needed for the conversion of soul that is required for knowledge of the Good; not even the "slow vegetable growth" fostered by paideia could be counted on to produce automatically the necessary turning of the soul. Perhaps these changes in paideia were rooted in massive changes in its social context. The Athenian *polis* lost its political integrity to Alexander's empire, to the empire's successor states, and then to Rome. Paideia had no further role as the education of citizens for a self-governing city. What it could offer was an education in inward happiness in the midst of outer social and political oppression and conflict. In any case, whatever the reason, the pagan paideia that Christians knew had itself "become a religion and an article of faith."[13]

For educated Greek-speaking people in the first century A.D., "culture" simply *was,* in a broad sense, paideia. When some of them became Christians, whether from pagan families or from Jewish families assimilated to Hellenistic culture, they came to Christianity as persons who had already been schooled in this way. It was unavoidable that they would construe their new Christian faith as an alternative paideia. Thus Clement of Rome, writing pastorally in A.D. 90 to the church in Corinth when it was divided by controversy, used literary tropes and patterns of argument likely to sway people formed by traditional paideia, referred to the "paideia of God" and the "paideia of Christ," and explicitly associated his letter with paideia to make it clear that the letter was to be read as a piece of Christian education.[14]

13. Jaeger, *Paideia,* 2:72.
14. Jaeger, *Early Christianity and Greek Paideia,* p. 25.

Presumably an analogous approach to pagans would be effective as a way to commend the faith: "Christianity's not so alien; it's a paideia like yours, aiming at the same goal, but superior in the way it does so."

Almost a century and a half after Clement of Rome, Clement of Alexandria and his brilliant student Origen were self-consciously affirming, not that Christianity was *like* paideia, not that it could simply make use of received paideia, but that Christianity *is* paideia, given by God in Jesus Christ, turning on a radical conversion possible only by the Holy Spirit's help, and taught only indirectly by study of divinely inspired Scriptures in the social context of the church understood to be in some ways a school. Thus, very early in the history of Christianity, paideia was simply built into the very way in which Christianity was understood by Christians themselves.

That is the historical reason why Christian theological education in North America is so deeply committed to "Athens" as a normative type of education. If Christianity is seen as a paideia, as it has been in its most ancient traditions, then it is simply a theological education whose goal is knowledge of God and, correlatively, forming persons' souls to be holy. However else theological education may come to be conceived — say, more narrowly as the education of clergy — it nonetheless will simply be a mode or variation of the paideia that Christianity itself more broadly is.

Thus far we have only shown the deep historical roots of this type or model of excellent education, which survived the massive cultural and intellectual changes introduced into Christianity in the eighteenth century by the European Enlightenment and continued to be an influential model in the modern period. After a sketch of the second type we shall return to examine a nineteenth-century version of the "Athens" model that has been particularly influential in the English-speaking world.

"Berlin"

The decision, reached after considerable controversy, to include a faculty of theology in the newly founded University of Berlin in 1810 created a new type of excellent theological education for which we shall let "Berlin" be the symbol. This type of education is bipolar: it stresses the interconnected importance of two quite different enterprises — *Wissenschaft* or orderly, disciplined critical research on the one hand, and "professional" education for ministry on the other. Several features characterize each of these interconnected poles. We can most quickly identify them through a brief sketch of the principles that shaped the original design of the University. They can then be abstracted into the artificial ahistorical type of excellent education that has in fact exercised hegemony over twentieth-century North American theological schooling.

Because the University of Berlin was deliberately designed to instantiate a newly emerged type of school, the "research university," it was an open question whether a theological faculty had any proper place in it. The University was founded as part of a reform of the Prussian educational system following Prussia's defeat by Napoleon, and it reflected a broader movement throughout Europe to reshape education along Enlightenment principles.[15] For a few months in 1809 and 1810 Wilhelm von Humboldt was head of the Prussian government's section on cultural and educational affairs, and he appointed a three-person committee, including theologian Friedrich Schleiermacher, to help him draft provisional statutes for a new university in Berlin.

15. Cf. Daniel Fallon, *The German University* (Boulder: Colorado Assoc. University Press, 1980); and Freidrich Paulsen, *The German Universities and University Study,* trans. F. Thilly and W. W. Elang (New York: Charles Scribner's Sons, 1906).

Schleiermacher wrote the founding document. The overarching and organizing goal of the university was to be research and teaching students how to do research; its goal was to be inquiry that aims to master the truth about whatever subject is studied. The only degree this university would award was the doctorate, the research degree. Only scholars who had published important research beyond the doctorate could be considered for faculty appointments. Only full professors would be considered members of the various faculties of the university. Whereas secondary schools teach students knowledge that is well established and no longer problematical, research universities, in Humboldt's words, "always treat knowledge as an as yet unresolved problem, and thus always stay at research."[16] The "Berlin" type of excellence in theological education can fairly be said to be part of Schleiermacher's enormously important theological legacy. However, even Schleiermacher had to make a case for including theology in the new research university; it was not self-evident that it should be so.

The reason for this lies in the very idea of "research." What is definitive of the research university is the sort of inquiry to which it is dedicated. Paideia, after all, also involved inquiry, especially into texts (classically, Homer; then also the poets; then the philosophers, especially Plato), the study of which was deemed to be the indirect way to come to know the Good itself. It was in its own way "critical": it involved testing what was studied for clarity, logical validity, and coherence. However, the inquiry that paideia calls for begins with the assumption of the authority of certain texts in regard to both secular and sacred matters. Notably, the alleged antiquity of a text was enough to establish its authority. Inquiry in a research university, by contrast, is far more radically *critical* in that it begins by requiring justification of all alleged

16. Humboldt, quoted in Fallon, p. 17.

authorities or bases for truth.[17] In principle, neither the antiquity of an opinion, nor the esteem of persons who hold the opinion, nor alleged divine inspiration alone justifies acceptance of any opinion as an authority. Furthermore, such inquiry is *disciplined* in the sense that it is highly self-conscious about the methods that are used to establish the truth about whatever is under study. These methods must provide ways rigorously to test and test again any claim to have discovered the truth about the subject under study, and the tests must be shown to be appropriate to the sort of thing being studied and to the sort of questions being asked about it. Moreover, such inquiry is *orderly* in that it seeks to locate its subject matter in the context of the largest possible set of relations to other things. Such inquiry is marked by a strong drive to build all-encompassing theories within which the interrelationships among all things can be traced. Orderly, disciplined, critical inquiry of this sort is the *Wissenschaft* (often misleadingly translated into English as "science") that makes a research university genuinely a place of *research*. On this model only the results of inquiry that is *wissenschaftlich* can count as "knowledge."

Theology's place in a research university was in doubt because theology had traditionally rested on "revelation," on authorities whose authoritative status could not itself be examined in an orderly, disciplined, and critical way. That theology was problematic is evident because of three characteristics of the research university that flow from its making *Wissenschaft* its defining goal. For one thing, in a research university *Wissenschaft* was united to teaching. Theological education had always involved teaching in the way paideia does — that is, teaching aims at indirectly cultivating capacities for knowing God. In a research university, however, teaching is aimed at cultivating capacities to do research, to engage in *Wissenschaft*. The research university

17. See Farley, *The Fragility of Knowledge,* chaps. 1 and 5.

was not to be simply a research center; it was to be a teaching institution — teaching not just the results of critical inquiry but also how to engage in critical inquiry so as to advance genuine knowledge. How could the sort of teaching appropriate to theology be united to this sort of inquiry, to *Wissenschaft?*

Furthermore, the hegemony of theology in the university had been explicitly overthrown. From the rise of the institution of the university in the Middle Ages onward, because of its base in divine revelation theology had been the highest and dominant faculty, superior to the faculties of arts and sciences and to the faculties of law and medicine, for theology was the "queen of the sciences" whom all other inquiries ultimately served. In the research university the basis of theology's claim to overarching authority was not recognized, and in effect the faculties of arts and sciences were made dominant. Granted, disestablishment does not necessarily mean eviction. Nonetheless, so radical a restructuring of power in the university left it very unclear whether theology still had any role in it.

Third, essential to a research university is the protection of academic freedom. "Freedom to learn" *(Lernfreiheit)* and "Freedom to teach" *(Lehrfreiheit)* are its central mottos. This was a deliberate rejection of theology's right in traditional universities, by virtue of being the superior faculty and often by virtue of civil law, to be the final court of appeal, and hence the ultimate censor, of what could be learned and taught. To include theology in a research university could easily seem a betrayal of the educational revolution that the research university represented.

Schleiermacher had an answer to these objections, and his successful argument for including a theology faculty in the University of Berlin added a second pole to the "Berlin" type of excellent theological education: Theological education should be included as "professional" education. His argument is partly sociological and partly philosophical-theological. The sociological argument is that every human society has sets of practices dealing with bodily health, social order, and religious needs. These are socially necessary practices — necessary, that is, for the well-being of society as a whole. Each of these practices requires properly trained leadership. Leadership will be properly trained only if it is given the best possible education. Therefore, a research university like the University of Berlin ought to include faculties of medicine, law, and theology in order to contribute to the well-being of society as a whole. A theology faculty ought to be included, as Edward Farley summarizes the argument, "to give cognitive and theoretical foundations to an *indispensable practice.*"[18]

Schleiermacher's argument thus far seems to leave him in a bind. If we agree with him, he has given a strong sociological reason for including theology in a research university; but the very notion of a research university seems necessarily to exclude theology.

Schleiermacher attempts to ease that bind with the philosophical-theological side of his argument. He agrees with his opponents that Christian theology is not a "pure" science. That is, its principles do not derive from universal principles that are available to any inquirer. Therefore, he agrees, theology is not an inquiry that can be included in the arts and sciences, which attend only to "pure" sciences. Theology, he stresses, is rooted in something specifically historical and cultural — the Christian church — rather than in universal principles. It is a "positive" science — that is, it is rooted in something historically simply "given" (or "posited"). Schleiermacher grants all of this to his opponents.

However, he then argues, it is precisely those features of theology that make it a possible subject of inquiry in a research university. The fact that a research university necessarily sets aside

18. Farley, *Theologia,* p. 86.

any subject's claim to rest on revealed principles that cannot themselves be the subject of critical inquiry poses no serious problem because, Schleiermacher argues on *philosophical* grounds, religions like Christianity do not rest on principles in the first place, revealed or otherwise. They rest on a kind of intuition or insightful experience, which can be the subject of philosophical inquiry. Hence Christian theology can be a subject of *wissenschaftlich* inquiry without threat of compromise either of Christianity's integrity or of the integrity of the university.

In the first place, the word *Christian* may be used descriptively to name a great array of historical and cultural phenomena called "Christian churches" and "Christian practices" and "Christian teachings" and "Christian texts" (including the Bible). These may all be researched *historically.* Schleiermacher called this "historical theology."

Second, the word *Christian* may be used normatively to designate that which is authentically Christian. What are the criteria of that? To answer that question, the results of historical study of Christianity can be subjected to *philosophical* analysis to determine the essence of Christianity, that which defines it and yields criteria by which to assess any particular teaching, institution, or practice that claims to be "Christian." Schleiermacher called this "philosophical theology."

Third, the results of the first two *wissenschaftlich* forms of critical inquiry can be put to work to determine the normative *rules* for carrying out the tasks of specifically Christian ministry.[19] Schleiermacher called this "practical theology," and he saw it as a *theoretical* undertaking, attending to normative rules implicit in authentically Christian practice. This brings the description of

---

19. Edward Farley has come up with the best characterization of Schleiermacher's picture of "practical theology": the "normative field which critically apprehends the *rules* for carrying out the tasks of ministry" (*Theologia*, p. 91).

theology in the research university back from research to "professional" education. Thus in practical theology the socially indispensable practice of church leadership is given cognitive and theoretical foundation by *Wissenschaft* (historical and philosophical theology). Theology can be included in a research university, but only by maintaining the interdependence between education for *Wissenschaft* and professional education. This bipolarity is the central structure of the "Berlin" type of excellent theological education.

For historical reasons, North American Christian theological education has come to be as inescapably committed to the "Berlin" type of excellent education as it is to the "Athens" type. This is a result of the history through which the model provided by the University of Berlin came to dominate American standards of higher education generally. Historians of American higher education generally point to the founding in 1876 of Johns Hopkins University, the first graduate university in the United States, as the moment when the "Berlin" model became decisive for American higher education. The Ph.D. degree it awarded was based on the German Dr. phil. degree, the research degree that was the highest degree awarded by a German faculty of arts and sciences. By 1884 virtually all of Johns Hopkins's faculty had studied in Germany, and thirteen had been awarded German doctorates. During the last third of the nineteenth century the research university exemplified by the University of Berlin became the normative model of excellence in higher education of all sorts in the United States. "Throughout this period of birth and development of the American university," Daniel Fallon writes, "the dominant influence, the overriding ideal, was the model of Humboldt's enlightenment university."[20]

The influence of this development in higher education on

20. Fallon, p. 52.

theological education was indirect and subtle. Theological schools in North America in this period did not turn into research universities. Most theological education had been and continued to be done in freestanding institutions making no claims to be versions of research universities. However, the "Berlin" type of excellent schooling did dictate prevailing standards of academically respectable education, which theological education embraced and to which it has held itself accountable. This is evident in many ways: in standards for academic accreditation, in research expectations of faculty, in attitudes toward the importance of library holdings, in privileging seminars as a way of teaching, etc. We shall see in Chapter 3 how the "Berlin" type has been modified in America, and how the modifications have introduced serious theological incoherences into theological education. What is important to stress here is simply that those modifications could not have generated such deep-seated problems had American theological education not so thoroughly conformed itself to the "Berlin" type of excellent education.

"Athens" and "Berlin"

In the examination that follows of five voices in the recent discussions of what is theological about theological education I shall use "Athens" and "Berlin" as types, as ahistorical and artificial constructs around which to organize the analysis. Each has implications different from the other regarding a number of features of education. It will be useful to draw them out here before using the two types to analyze current proposals about theological education.

According to the "Athens" model, theological education is a movement from source to personal appropriation of the source, from revealed wisdom to the appropriation of revealed wisdom in a way that is identity forming and personally transforming. This is true whether theological education is understood broadly as education in "the faith" or more narrowly as education for church leadership. In either case, it is understood that appropriation does not come about through direct instruction. Rather, it comes about indirectly by inquiry into other matters whose study is believed to capacitate persons to appropriate this wisdom for themselves. This means that theological education of the "Athens" type tends to focus on the student, on helping the student undergo a deep kind of formation. To be sure, study focuses on various subject matters. However, this study is ordered to something more basic, the students' own personal appropriation of wisdom about God and about themselves in relation to God.

This has implications for the relationship between teacher and learner. It must be an indirect relationship. Teachers themselves are also seeking personally to appropriate wisdom about God and about themselves in relation to God. At most, the teacher "teaches" only indirectly by providing a context in which the learner may come to that combined self-knowledge and God-knowledge that *is* a "personal appropriation" of revealed wisdom. Central to this context are those texts and practices, such as Scripture and the practice of the Christian life, whose study is believed to lead to understanding God.

This, in turn, has implications regarding who is qualified to teach in theological education on the "Athens" model. There are two very different sorts of capacities required to do such teaching. One is extraordinary learning in regard to the relevant texts and practices. The other is a set of personal gifts for the indirect "teaching" that, as midwife, helps another come to personal appropriation of revealed wisdom. The two sets of qualifications are in tension with each other, and the tension creates the possibility of serious deformity in this type of education. If "learnedness" is overstressed, education tends to slip into direct communication of information, subverting the basic character of this type of education. On the other hand, if the personal gifts for this sort of teaching are overstressed, education tends to slip into manipulation or therapy, technique tends to become dominant, and the substance by which the student was indirectly to be "formed" gets lost.

All of this has implications regarding the communal context of education. Theological education of the "Athens" type is inherently communal. The learning is in one way "individualistic," in that each must do it for herself or himself. Yet, by definition it cannot be solitary. Teachers and learners together constitute a community sharing the common goal of personally appropriating revealed wisdom. It is, then, a community ordered to the same end, a community under orders. Some members of the community, presumably the teachers, have been engaged in this common quest longer than others, presumably the learners; but it is a shared quest.

Theological education on the "Athens" model is, finally, a public undertaking — though it is "public" in a qualified sense. We saw that paideia, both in its most ancient form and in its Platonic revision, was ordered to public life in the sense of political activity in the public realm, while in its Hellenistic form it had become ordered to the private realm of individual inward religiosity. Christian theological education on the "Athens" model can be ordered to either sort of end. It depends on differing theological judgments about the nature of Christianity. Those judgments are themselves the substance of theological reflection in the course of theological education, and they are not dictated by the "Athens" model itself. So in one sense of the term *public,* theological education of the "Athens" type may not be a public undertaking but rather would be intensely inward and private. In another sense of the term, however, even that privatistic version would also necessarily be public. It would be public in the sense that it cannot be arcane. Because it is education that must proceed indirectly by way of the examination of texts and practices whose study is believed to lead to understanding God and all else in relation to God, and because those texts and practices employ ordinary languages belonging to widely shared cultures and do themselves have cultural locations, such education is inescapably a public undertaking, understandable to anyone who understands the relevant languages and cultures. Theological education of the "Athens" type is unavoidably done in public and is unavoidably engaged in self-conscious cultural transactions with its host culture.

According to the "Berlin" model, theological education is a movement from data to theory to application of theory to practice. This movement correlates with its bipolar structure: *Wissenschaft* for critical rigor in theorizing; "professional" education for rigorous study of the application of theory in practice.

This type is open to important variations, and therefore to important confusions, at three points. First, "professional" can be understood in a variety of ways in theological education. Second, there can be a variety of judgments about what forms of *Wissenschaft* are relevant for theological education. For instance, it is not logically necessary to this type that one of the required kinds of critical inquiry be a philosophical quest for the "essence" of Christianity (or of anything else); the type is fully compatible, for example, with a philosophical judgment that the project of hunting for "essences" is itself misguided. Most important of all, there can be very different judgments about how the relevant *Wissenschaft* pole is related to the "professional" pole. In Chapter 3 we will review a series of modifications that twentieth-century North American theological education has made in the "Berlin" type, and we will note confusions and incoherences that some of those changes have promoted.

Nonetheless, in all its variations, theological education of the "Berlin" type rests on direct communication. The *Wissenschaft* pole requires that study focus on the research project. Critical inquiry focuses simultaneously on questions about the subject being researched and on questions about the methods of research that are required both by the questions the researchers are asking of the subject matter and by the character of the subject matter itself. Different methods are required if one is asking sociologist's rather than chemist's questions about an ancient artifact; and still other methods are required if the artifact in question is a text written on bone rather than on bronze. Both what research involves and what it discovers must be communicated directly by teachers to students. So too, the professional pole, as Schleiermacher envisioned it, requires direct communication. The largely implicit rules that normatively govern specifically "Christian" practice, and in particular ministerial practice, can be identified, tested for their conformity with the essence of Christianity (which philosophical theology discovers in the *Wissenschaft* pole), and communicated to students, all quite directly.

This has implications for the relation between teacher and learner. The teacher does not exist *for* the student, as is the case in paideia. Instead, the teacher is basically a researcher who needs the student to help achieve the goal of research in a cooperative enterprise. Humboldt said that this cooperation proceeds by "combining a practiced mind, which is on that very account apt to be more one-sided and less active [the teacher's] with one which, though weaker and still neutral, bravely attempts every possibility [the student's]."[21]

Given the bipolar structure of the "Berlin" type, this has a further implication for theological education that is of momentous importance. When theological education conforms to the "Berlin" type of education, what makes it *theological* is its pro-

21. Humboldt, quoted in Paulsen, p. 53.

fessional pole, not its *Wissenschaft* pole. The *Wissenschaft* pole is governed by research agendas, by sets of topics to be researched. For Schleiermacher it was to be a historian's research agenda, followed by a philosopher's agenda. Biblical texts, church institutions, practices of worship, moral standards, and the like are all equally to be studied to discover their origins, how and why they changed through time, what their influences have been, etc. Then, of that entire, utterly heterogeneous array of phenomena, the question of their underlying Christian "essence" was to be asked. Inquiry is governed, not, as in the "Athens" type, by an interest thereby indirectly to come to know God, but by an interest to discover as directly as possible the truth about the origin, effects, and essential nature of "Christian" phenomena.

There is nothing "theological" about all of that. Nor need there be. Neither intuitive experience of God nor capacities for such experience are cultivated, not even indirectly, by engaging in *Wissenschaft*. Such experience is cultivated only in religious communities of whose inward experience all these Christian phenomena are but outward expressions. What makes theological education of the "Berlin" type *theological* is that it aims at preparing leaders for just those communities, leaders capacitated to help those communities nurture consciousness of God.

Note, then, that what makes theological education of this type *theological* is that it is ordered, not theocentrically, but ecclesiocentrically — to understanding church, or more exactly, to understanding church leadership, not to understanding God. There may be excellent theological reasons for adopting just this view; at this point it is important simply to note what the view is. Note secondly a deep irony in the "Berlin" type of excellence in theological education: Although what makes it properly "theological" is its goal (as "professional" education) of nurturing the health of the church by preparing for it excellent leadership, what entitles it to a home in the *wissenschaftlich* education it needs is

24

the rather different goal of nurturing the health of society as a whole (for which professional church leadership is a "necessary practice").

Clearly, this has important implications regarding faculty. The major criteria governing selection of persons for faculty positions in accord with this type of theological education is not simply great learning in already established knowledge, but demonstrated capacity to engage in scholarly research; and it is not so much personal capacities to be midwife of others' coming to an understanding of God and of themselves in relation to God as it is the ability to cultivate capacities for scholarly research in others. The normal way of demonstrating capacity for research, of course, is by publication of results of critical inquiry that make original contributions to the fund of knowledge.

Theological education on the "Berlin" model is, finally, a public undertaking in two ways that are in some tension with each other. It is public in a sense in which education on the "Athens" model is also: it is publicly accessible to any interested person who has the necessary competencies. Indeed, as the result of disciplined and orderly critical inquiry, it is supposed to be accessible independent of any prejudices or special interests of either the researcher or the competent observer. On the other hand, as "professional" education for a socially necessary practice, it is public in the sense of contributing to public welfare, the general good. As the latter, it cannot help but be engaged in major policies confronting society as a whole. If either of these two senses of "public" is stressed to the disadvantage of the other, theological education on this model is in danger of becoming either under- or over-engaged in social and cultural controversies of the day.

Perhaps the deepest difference between the two types comes, ironically, at the point at which they seem most alike. At the founding of the University of Berlin, Humboldt was explicit in saying that, in making the faculty of arts and sciences central, the research university had the same overarching goal as that of ancient Athens' paideia: it "transforms the character." However, he did not note a major difference between the underlying picture of human being assumed by paideia and that assumed by the Enlightenment research university.

The difference comes out in two ways. It comes out, first, when one asks on what basis education would have this character-transforming effect. Friedrich Paulsen observed that it would have this effect "not on the basis of medieval church unity," nor, we must add, on the basis of Hellenistic culture's view of what makes the good life, "but rather on the basis of the unity of human civilization and scientific work, the unity based on the modern ideal of humanity."[22]

Second, the difference between the views of human being underlying our two types is brought out when we ask about this "modern ideal of humanity." This "ideal" is the Enlightenment view of humanity, at the heart of which is a particular view of human rationality that is quite different from that assumed by the "Athens" model of education. At the core of the view of human being underlying paideia and the "Athens" model is the view that *the* characteristic defining human being is the capacity of reason in intuitive, cognitive judgment to apprehend the ultimate principle of being and of value — that is, God. This intuitive act is the very heart of rationality; it is the act of knowing that provides the foundation for all other knowing. By contrast, at the core of the view of human being underlying *Wissenschaft* in its relation to ministerial practice in the "Berlin" model is the view that *the* characteristic defining human being is reason's capacity to test and if necessary correct any and all "intuitions" — that is, its capacity to engage in disciplined and orderly critical inquiry.

22. Paulsen, p. 54.

If there is a human capacity for intuitive experience of God, the intuition is not necessarily irrational, but it is a-rational. It is not genuinely "cognitive"; it does not yield "knowledge," strictly speaking. Only after critical testing do we have true "knowledge." "Intellectual intuition" and "reason" are strictly separated, and only human capacities for critical, disciplined, orderly problem solving in the framework of research agendas, or other situations approximating such research agendas, count as "rationality."

*   *   *

The central project in this book is to examine critically a body of literature that grew up in the 1980s concerning theological education and what is theological about it. I shall organize the discussion around an axis whose poles are our two normative types of theological education. These two types are of varying ages — the "Berlin" type of excellent Christian theological education only emerged in the early nineteenth century, while the "Athens" type had emerged by the end of the first Christian century. But both types had undergone important modifications by the mid-twentieth century. Consequently it will be important to locate the recent discussion by noting major ways in which the versions of each type that the current discussion received had been materially modified. In the next chapter I shall present a case study of a mid-nineteenth-century version of the "Athens" type that was highly honored, at least verbally, in some mid-twentieth-century discussions of higher education generally, in order to draw attention to ways in which the material modifications it introduced have proved to be problematic. Then in Chapter 3 I shall review a series of proposals about specifically theological education in the first half of the twentieth century in the United States that accord with the "Berlin" type but make important and equally problematic modifications in it.

2

"Athens" in the Mid-Nineteenth Century

The rise of the research university as the "Berlin" type of excellent education did not simply displace "Athens" as a type of excellent schooling in European and American higher education in the nineteenth century. Indeed, the English-speaking world by and large simply continued to assume that higher education at its best is defined by "Athens." Oxford and Cambridge, probably the most prestigious universities in the English-speaking world, long resisted the Continental research university model. In the United States, although some state universities and a few private universities explicitly adopted the "Berlin" type, the great majority of undergraduate education took place in liberal arts colleges that tacitly assumed "Athens" as the type of excellence to which they aspired. For historical reasons reviewed in the last chapter, Christian theological schools for the most part did the same.

Nonetheless, the fact that an alternative type now existed inevitably shaped the way in which the "Athens" type was understood. To the extent that educators, especially theological educators, self-consciously reflected on these matters, it was necessary to reflect on how their preferred "Athens" model differed from the Continental research university model of excellent education. "Athens" had to be understood in contradistinction to "Berlin." And that led to shifts in emphasis in and material modifications of the "Athens" type.

John Henry Newman's *The Idea of a University*

These subtle but important modifications are particularly clear in what is probably the intellectually most powerful modern reformulation of the "Athens" type, John Henry Cardinal Newman's *The Idea of a University*.[1] This work, which consists of a series of lectures first published in 1852, almost half a century after the founding of the University of Berlin, is an enormously influential classic in the controversial literature about the nature and purposes of higher education. It has shaped the guiding vision of much education conducted under Roman Catholic and Anglican auspices, and it has set the terms on which advocates of the alternative "Berlin" type of educational excellence have often been required to argue their case. Its concern is undergraduate education, including undergraduate theological education, and it is explicitly not concerned with ministerial education.

Nonetheless, Newman's lectures are worth examining as a reminder of the particularly modern, post-"Berlin" *shape* of the "Athens" type that continues, almost entirely tacitly and implicitly, to give form to much twentieth-century American theological education. The version of the "Athens" type of educational ex-

---

1. Newman, *The Idea of a University* (New York: Longmans, Green and Co., 1899).

cellence that Newman develops does powerfully express the assumptions about excellence in theological education that continue to be implicit in much seminary schooling in the twentieth century. Furthermore, Newman's modification of the "Athens" type has strong parallels with some proposals in the current conversations concerning what is "theological" about theological education.

At the same time, Newman's lectures are instructive in a cautionary kind of way. Newman's modifications of the "Athens" type are theologically problematic. His social assumptions, his view of human rationality, and his vision of the fulfilled human life are so alien to North American culture in the late twentieth century that they may help to distance us from our own assumptions about social values, human rationality, and the fulfilled life. At the same time, his historical and cultural distance from us may help to highlight features of the "Athens" type that are inherently worrisome when the type is adopted by specifically theological education. Examination of Newman's essay, then, can both clarify one side of current American theological education's legacy (the shape the "Athens" type tends to take following the creation of the research university) and draw out problems it creates for theological education that embraces it.

With papal backing, Newman was in the midst of a campaign in Ireland to found a Roman Catholic university there. There seemed to be local support for the project since, at the time, Roman Catholic students could not obtain a university-level education except at a Protestant institution. However, conservative elements in the hierarchy and clergy desired ecclesiastical control over teaching to guarantee that it would produce educated Catholics. Newman opposed such ecclesiastical control.

Perhaps it was tactical considerations in that setting that dictated the structure of the lectures. They divide into two parts. In the first four lectures Newman takes up the question of the inner unity of the various subjects to be taught in the university. He argues that theology must play a central role in unifying the subjects taught. *That* ought to reassure the conservatives! However, on closer inspection it becomes clear that what makes university studies a single course of study and not simply a clutch of courses is the overall goal of teaching them, namely (for Newman) the cultivation of students' intellectual capacities to the point of excellence, and cultivating these capacities for their own sake. That line of thought is not developed until the last four chapters. The order of exposition reverses the logical order of Newman's ideas. That is, the grounds for the arguments in the first four lectures are developed only in the last four. It is in the pivotal fifth chapter that Newman makes clear that the series breaks down into these two halves. It is illuminating to examine Newman's hunt for *the* Idea (or essence) of a university by considering the two halves of his lecture series in reverse.

Teaching Students

Newman ties the unity of a university to its one overarching *purpose*. "The view taken of a University in these Discourses," Newman wrote in his preface to the published lectures, "is the following: — That it is a place of *teaching* universal *knowledge*."[2] Given this view, as he points out in the pivotal fifth discourse, "a University may be considered with reference either to its Students or to its Studies" (99).

Note that it is Newman's picture of the overarching goal of teaching students and not the prevailing self-definition of academic specialties that controls his picture of how diverse fields may be integrated in a single curriculum. What is cautionary is

2. Newman, p. ix; subsequent citations will be made parenthetically in the text.

Newman's unself-critically abstract way of linking "teaching studies" and "teaching students."

Newman explains the overarching goal of teaching by reference to those who are taught, not by reference to what is taught. By this move he embraces paideia as the model of excellence in schooling. However, it is a modified paideia because his view of human rationality is different from the view classically assumed by paideia. The goal of teaching "is simply the cultivation of the intellect, as such, and its object is nothing more or less than intellectual excellence" (121). More exactly, what is cultivated is an array of capacities and powers. They are "intellectual" in that they are capacities we exercise in knowing.

> We know, not by a direct and simple vision, not at a glance, but, as it were, by piecemeal and accumulation, by a mental process, by going round an object, by the comparison, the combination, the mutual correction, the continual adaptation, of many partial notions, by the employment, concentration, and joint action of many faculties and exercises of mind. (151)

Newman stresses the role of these capacities in actively forming knowledge. Learning brings a sense of enlightenment or enlargement. However,

> the enlargement consists, not merely in the passive reception into the mind of a number of ideas hitherto unknown to it, but in the mind's energetic and simultaneous action upon and towards and among those new ideas, which are rushing in upon it. It is the action of a formative power, reducing to order and meaning the matter of our acquirements. (134; cf. 74-75)

The overarching goal for which a university exists is to cultivate these capacities in its students to the point of excellence by skilled teaching. Newman's notion of intellectual excellence is

33

analogous to a traditional understanding of moral excellence as "virtue." But it is only analogous, not identical. Here he departs from the classical paideia model for which, as we said, cultivation of the mind's excellence was identical with coming to an intuitive grasp of the Good. It involved a conversion of the person. Intellectual and moral excellence are one. For Newman they are only analogous.

A moral virtue is a *habitus,* a settled disposition of the will to act habitually in a morally excellent way — courageously, faithfully, honestly, prudently, etc. By analogy, Newman suggests, intellectual excellence is a kind of "perfection or virtue of the intellect," which he elects to call by the name of "philosophy" (125) or "a philosophical habit of mind" (51). It is important not to be misled by his archaic use of these terms. For us "philosophy" commonly names either an array of questions and intellectual problems or a body of literature generated by discussing such questions and problems. For Newman philosophy is not only a habit of mind but the habit whose acquisition is the highest fulfillment of the mind. It is taught by exercising students' intellectual capacities under discipline until they acquire the requisite habits (cf. 152). What are these habits? Breadth of mind; the capacity to set every topic and question in a larger relevant frame of reference; clarity of thought and expression; fair-minded even-handedness in assessing conflicting arguments; rigorous criticism in assessing "the dense mass of facts and events";[3] and, most important of all for Newman, "judgment," that "master-principle . . . which gives [a person] strength in any subject . . . to *seize the strong point* in it" (174).

Newman's major polemical thrust in these lectures is the stress that, even though it does not have the widest possible public utility, this unifying goal is its *own end* pursued for its own sake.

3. Newman, p. 138; cf. pp. 137-38, 174, and pp. xi-xii, xvi-xviii.

Pursuing it — that is, actually doing university education — cannot be justified by showing that it is necessary to the achievement of any further end. This is the basis of Newman's opposition to ecclesiastical control of the university. Against the conservative elements in the hierarchy and clergy, Newman vigorously insisted that the purpose of cultivating the intellect of students lay in the cultivation itself and not in any further desirable end, neither in sanctity nor in moral goodness:

> Liberal Education makes not the Christian, not the Catholic, but the gentleman. It is well to be a gentleman, it is well to have a cultivated intellect, a delicate taste, a candid, equitable, dispassionate mind, a noble and courteous bearing in the conduct of life; — these are the connatural qualities of a large knowledge; they are the objects of a University; I am advocating, I shall illustrate and insist upon them; but still, I repeat, they are no guarantee for sanctity or even for conscientiousness, they may attach to the man of the world, to the profligate, to the heartless, — pleasant, alas, and attractive as he shows when decked out in them.[4]

Here the differences between Newman's view of human reason and that of paideia show themselves plainly. It was central to paideia that the cultivation of human reason would, contrary to Newman, inherently yield not merely the "gentleman" but the good person. What is questionable in Newman's proposal is the view of human personhood that underlies the content of his theory of teaching.

Newman's closeness to classical paideia surfaces again in his insistence that a university ought not to house research or professional education. The end of teaching is the cultivation of the intellect, not the accumulation of new knowledge. To discover

---

4. Newman, pp. 120-21; cf. pp. xvi-xviii.

and to teach are distinct functions. They are also distinct gifts and are not commonly found united in the same person. For these reasons, Newman argued, teaching constitutes a university; let research and discovery constitute "academies" as distinct institutions (cf. ix).

Teaching pertinent to the several professions, on the other hand, does lie within the purview of university teaching, but *not* as "professional" education. Newman understands "professional" education as education that has as its end the cultivation of capacities useful to improve "the health of the body, or of the commonwealth, or of the soul" (108). Left at that, it tends toward the narrowing of the intellect rather than the enlargement that comes from teaching whose end is the cultivation of intellectual capacities as such without reference to their utility. But teaching pertinent to the professions need not be left at that.

> In saying that Law or Medicine is not the end of a University course, I do not mean to imply that the University does not teach Law or Medicine. What indeed can it teach at all, if it does not teach something particular? It teaches *all* knowledge by teaching all *branches* of knowledge, and in no other way. I do but say that there will be this distinction as regards a Professor of Law, or of Medicine . . . in a University and out of it, that out of a University he is in danger of being absorbed and narrowed by his pursuit, and of giving Lectures which are the Lectures of nothing more than a lawyer, physician, [etc.]; whereas in a University he will know just where he and his science stand, he has come to it, as it were, from a height, he has taken a survey of all knowledge, he is kept from extravagance by the very rivalry of other studies, he has gained from them a special illumination and largeness of mind and freedom and self-possession, and he treats his own in consequence with a philosophy and a resource, which belongs not to the study itself, but to his liberal education. (166-67)

Here Newman seems to be trying to draw a sharp and clear line between teaching theology (or law or medicine) as part of "professional" education and teaching it as one among many subjects in "university" education. He appears to draw between them a difference in principle grounded in fundamentally different goals. The goal of teaching theology in professional education is to prepare people to fill certain professional roles that are narrowly defined because they are defined by reference to the well-being of some one aspect of human being (health of the soul or health of the body or health of the commonwealth). By contrast, the goal of teaching theology in university education is the same broad goal that teaching any other subject has: to cultivate human intellectual capacities without regard to their utility, simply because they are valuable in themselves.

Nothing could be more contrary to the nineteenth-century research university model of excellent schooling than Newman's exclusion of research and professional schools from a university. His grounds for their exclusion are important: to include them is to compromise the defining goal of a university — that is, the cultivation of intellectual excellence for its own sake.

This does not mean that Newman denies any public significance to the university. To the contrary, he stresses its public role and importance. But the way in which he argues for the university's public role is very distinctive. University teaching is "training good members of society. Its art is the art of social life, and its end is fitness for the world" (177). This is not simply to claim that university education trains conscientious and informed citizen-voters. Rather, Newman is making the more ambitious claim that people educated in the university are prepared for responsible leadership in public affairs. University education prepares one "to fill any post with credit, and to master any subject with facility. . . . [One] is at home in any society [and] has common ground with every class." However, the university accomplishes this only indirectly. It prepares people for "any post" because of the sorts of capacities that university teaching directly cultivates for their own sakes: "a clear conscious view of [one's] own opinions and judgments, a truth in developing them, an eloquence in expressing them, a force in urging them" (178); a capacity to place issues in the broadest framework rather than being confined to the "views [of] particular professions" (177); critical capacities "to detect what is sophistical, and to discard what is irrelevant"; and above all, judgment, the capacity to "see things as they are, to go right to the point" (178). Although it trains excellent bureaucrats and government ministers, Newman's university plays this public role only indirectly. The public significance of university teaching arises precisely from its apparent *in*utility. Indeed, only if university teaching is done only for its own sake can it have its public significance as a by-product.

Thus far, then, Newman's view of university education is a version of paideia as the model of excellent schooling. Like paideia, it is schooling focused on shaping individual students' capacities simply for the sake of doing so and not for the sake of any utilitarian end. It is important to note that the way Newman develops these points rests on the notion that the capacities in question are specifically capacities of "reason" and that there is an "essence" to reason. Reason is one selfsame thing in all otherwise apparently diverse persons. Indeed, reason is understood to have nothing directly to do with "will"; cultivating the capacities of reason will not in itself develop moral virtue. This is a major part of Newman's revision of classical paideia, in which the connection between reason and will was so direct and immediate that to be capacitated to know the truth was identical with being capacitated to do the Good. Despite this important reformulation, Newman's model of excellent schooling is nonetheless recognizable as a version of paideia based on his discovery of the essence of reason. We shall see that the other half of his argument rests on this view and that it opens the door to some exceedingly dubious notions.

Teaching Subjects

Newman's essay is also instructive in a cautionary way when we shift attention from his last four lectures on "teaching students" to his first four on "teaching subjects." Precisely because in the last four lectures he is going to argue to a Roman Catholic audience that a Catholic university is rightly conceived only when it is *not* designed to nurture either sanctity or morality, he finds it useful to spend the first four lectures vigorously affirming that no university studies are adequately comprehensive or unified unless they include the study of theology. That, at any rate, is the explicit thesis of the first four lectures. By "theology" he means "the science of God," or what today might be called "foundational theology," and not Christian dogma or Christian practical theology. However, Newman is not arguing for either the material or the formal hegemony of theology. That is, he is not arguing that truth claims in all other subjects are answerable to or must be translated into theological claims. Nor is he arguing that the distinctive methods of theology as a "science" ought to be employed in other sciences.

Instead, Newman argues for the inclusion of theology on what we might call the "principle of comprehensiveness." If a university is a "place of teaching universal knowledge" (ix; emphasis omitted), it must include knowledge of God among the subjects taught or it is no longer truly comprehensive. In Newman's view, "all that exists, as contemplated by the human mind, forms one large system or complex fact, and this of course resolves itself into an indefinite number of particular facts." Human intellectual capacities cannot grasp the one large and complex fact as such. However, we can grasp subsets, as it were, of the indefinite

39

"particular facts" into which the "complex fact" resolves itself, taken "in their mutual positions and bearings" (45). Thus the several subjects taught in a university are aspects of the one "complex fact" that have been abstracted from it for convenience in teaching and learning. Each subject employs methods appropriate to the distinctive features of the subset of "facts" that comprises the aspect of the "complex fact" with which it deals. Indeed, it is a subject's peculiar methods of inquiry that constitute that subject as a science.

To be sure, Newman believes that all facts depend on their relation to God both for their coherence with one another and for their concrete actuality. God is the principle of unity in the universe. But the science of theology is *not* the principle of unity in the university. If any science fills that role, it is philosophy, whose task it is to comprehend "the bearings of one science upon another" and, within the one large system or complex fact, "the location and limitation and adjustment and due appreciation of them all, one with another" (51).

Theology must be included among the subjects taught in a university simply because it is dangerous to exclude it:

> I observe, then, that, if you drop any science out of the circle of knowledge, you cannot keep its place vacant for it; that science is forgotten; the other sciences close up, or, in other words, they exceed their proper bounds, and intrude where they have no right. (73)

If the principle of comprehensiveness is violated in a university and some subject — say, theology — is not taught, not only is some important abstractable aspect of the "one large system or complex fact" of truth absent, but each of the subjects that *is* included will inevitably be distorted.

Once again we observe Newman making his case for his version of paideia as excellent schooling by basing it on the results of a hunt for an essence. In this case the "essence" in question is the grandest essence of all, the underlying structure of reality that unifies the vast multitude of kinds of things into one universe. For Plato the Good filled this role. Newman prefers to call it "Truth." It is because Truth grounds the multiplex universe as one "complex fact" that no single aspect of it, not even God, may be left out of the study of the universe.

Given Newman's conception of the unity of truth, this conclusion may follow cogently enough. But why does it matter? Why could not the unifying goal of university teaching be accomplished as well by cultivating students' intellectual capacities through teaching partially distorted subjects as through teaching properly located and defined subjects? Couldn't one achieve the same goal teaching *anything?* No, because of the specific character of the goal that teaching seeks for its own sake: intellectual excellence. As we have seen, intellectual excellence centers on capacities to *locate* critically and clearly each subject matter in the broadest possible frame of reference. It is impossible to cultivate such capacities by teaching students when the principle of comprehensiveness is violated in the selection of subjects taught.

Critique

As we have seen, Newman has derived the unity of a university's curriculum from the goal of its teaching. Granted, coherence among the several sciences that constitute the subjects taught in a university corresponds to the coherence of reality or, as Newman prefers to put it, Truth. That is, the unity of the sciences is warranted by Newman's metaphysical vision. However, their place *and* unity precisely as a university's course of study are warranted only by reference to the goal of university *teaching* — that is, the cultivation for its own sake of intellectual excellence. Neither place nor unity is grounded in considerations of method of inquiry. No one science's method is granted hegemony such that a subject matter can demonstrate its right to be part of the university curriculum merely by displaying its use of a privileged "scientific method." Nor may the unity of the curriculum be achieved by negotiations among subjects that autonomously define their own methods and agendas. Rather, sciences are licensed to a place in the curriculum by the demonstrable connection between teaching them as subjects, on the one hand, and the cultivation of students' intellectual capacities and the enlargement or breadth of their frames of reference, on the other. Diverse subjects are unified into a single course of studies precisely by the end to which they are taught: the cultivation of intellectual excellence. We may find Newman's metaphysical vision and his view of the unity of truth problematical, but his way of relativizing methods of inquiry and the pretensions of subject matter to central importance while finding a source of unity for a school's intellectual work is instructive.

The material difficulties with Newman's entire project, however, are urgent. They are generated by the distinct type of abstractness that affects Newman's thinking — namely, a theorizing about university teaching that is entirely abstracted from the concrete cultural setting of the "values" judged to characterize intellectual excellence and deemed worthy of cultivating for their own sake. These values are celebrated in total abstraction from any consideration of the concrete social setting of the actual lives of those who are to be educated, and also in abstraction from any consideration of the concrete setting of Newman himself. We have learned from the hermeneutics of suspicion to suspect such abstractions of being "innocent theorizing" — innocent, that is, of any self-suspicion that they might be ideologically skewed.

This abstractness is signaled by a passage we have already quoted:

> Liberal Education makes not the Christian, not the Catholic, but
> the gentleman. It is well to be a gentleman, it is well to have a
> cultivated intellect, a delicate taste, a candid, equitable, dis-
> passionate mind, a noble and courteous bearing in the conduct
> of life. . . . (120)

The virtues that constitute intellectual excellence turn out be
identical with the excellence that makes one a "gentleman." It is
a remarkable coincidence, and a troubling one. "Gentleman,"
after all, is a social status defined by very particular socioeconomic
conditions. In Newman's mid-nineteenth-century British setting,
it was a status limited to *(a)* males, who *(b)* were enfranchised to
vote, and whose material resources were large enough both *(c)* to
free them from the necessity of investing time and energy to
support themselves so that they might invest time and energy
providing leadership in public affairs, and *(d)* to free them from
narrow use of their intellectual capacities in commercial and
professional work so that instead they might enlarge their intellectual capacities for their own sake. One requires considerable
material resources to be sufficiently free from the practical
demands of the workaday world to be able to devote oneself to
cultivating intellect, a "delicate taste," a "candid, equitable, dis-
passionate mind," and a "noble and courteous bearing." Only
young men with access to such resources could afford Newman's
university teaching. It is not surprising that members of such a
class, including Newman himself, would select just those values
as the marks of an excellence worth cultivating for its own sake,
the excellence of a gentleman.

It is troubling that these values that mark the excellence of
a gentleman turn out also to be the virtues marking *intellectual*
excellence. The *identification* of the virtues that mark intellectual
excellence ought to be warranted, not by the accidents of socioeconomic status that privilege a few, but by a picture of human

rationality that applies to all persons. That is exactly what Newman claims to do. He thinks of human rationality as "the power
of viewing many things at once as one whole, of referring them
severally to their true place in the universal system, of understanding their respective values, and determining their mutual depen-
dence" (137). As we have seen, he holds that our capacities do
not empower us to view things as a whole all at once intuitively.
Rather, we build up this view of things "piecemeal" by a process
of "going round an object" and comparing, correcting, and combining "many partial notions" (151). Human rationality, then, is
a set of capacities for a process of ascent from a multitude of
particular and partial notions to more general and fundamental
principles that order those notions into a picture of things "as
one whole." "We must generalize, we must reduce to method, we
must have a grasp of principles, and group and shape our acqui-
sitions by means of them," Newman argues (139). Given this
picture of rationality, it follows that the virtues characterizing
intellectual excellence include clarity in generalization, even-
handedness and fairness in assessing conflicting arguments,
breadth of frame of reference in locating and interrelating facts,
and sound critical judgment in identifying fundamental principles. But why the remarkable coincidence that makes this *way*
of identifying intellectual virtue so troublingly like ideological
justification of the values of a cultural elite established by prevailing socioeconomic power arrangements?

The answer, I suggest, lies in a largely assumed view of the
essence of human nature that embraces Newman's more explicit
view of human rationality. There are two notable features of this
view of human personhood. First, the defining feature of specifically human being is the capacity to know by contemplation.
Newman cites Cicero to the effect that knowledge is "the very
first object to which we are attracted, after the supply of our
physical wants." The desire to supply physical wants, after all, is

common to all types of living beings. What is distinctive to human beings is "the pursuit of Knowledge for its own sake" (104). "Knowing," in turn, is consistently construed by Newman as a contemplative act, an act more like intellectual seeing than like bodily "doing" to accomplish a further end:

> for I suppose Science and Philosophy, in their elementary idea, are nothing else but this habit of *viewing,* as it may be called, the objects which sense conveys to the mind, of throwing them into system, and uniting and stamping them with one form. (75)

Furthermore, to say that we do this for its own sake is to say that "contemplative" seeing is enjoyable rather than fruitful for other ends. For this distinction Newman quotes Aristotle: "By fruitful, I mean, which yield revenue; by enjoyable, where *nothing accrues of consequence beyond the using.*"[5] Accordingly, an education suited precisely to the defining characteristic of our humanity will be a cultivation of contemplative capacities for knowing for its own sake and not for any practical utility. The overlap with paideia as a model for excellent schooling is obvious.

The second salient feature of this view of human personhood is the way in which it understands human sociality. According to this view, we are constituted by an intersubjectivity to which institutional structures are accidental and extraneous. It is not that Newman denies the reality of economic and political power arrangements, either in society as a whole or in a particular community like a school. Rather, such institutional realities have no intrinsic bearing on what it is to be a human person — nor, more particularly, on what it is to be rational. Such seems to be the assumption behind a curious passage in which Newman says that if he had to choose between a "so-called University" that

5. Newman, p. 109, quoting Aristotle, *Rhetoric* 1.5.

45

dispensed with a residential community and a university "which had no professors or examinations at all, but merely brought a number of young men together for three or four years, and then sent them away" (145), he would unhesitatingly choose the latter. Why? Because, entirely in the absence of any institutional structures, human intersubjectivity is such that the "youthful community will constitute a whole. . . . It will give birth to a living teaching, which in course of time will take the shape of a self-perpetuating tradition, or a *genius loci* . . . which imbues and forms, more or less, and one by one, every individual who is successively brought under its shadow" (147). That human persons are social animals is manifested in the creation of traditions; but, Newman seems to assume, traditions can be understood independently of concrete structuring of social power.

In this view, human persons are not understood as agents sharing a public space defined by the structure and dynamics of political, economic, and social power but as contemplators sharing a space defined by an intellectual tradition that is independent of the realities of social power. If human agency is subordinated to contemplation in the essential structure of human being, it is not surprising that Newman should separate cultivation of capacities for contemplation from active research, nor that he should separate education of the intellect from moral formation. If contemplative capacities are more basic to our humanity than are competencies for intentional action, it is not surprising that Newman's idea of teaching should privilege intellectual values that correlate with political, economic, and social privilege. Nor is it surprising that his idea of teaching, while focusing on critical capacities, does not call for self-critical capacities. It is a picture of human being that comports all too comfortably with the socially privileged, whose lives can be ordered by values that apparently (but only apparently) transcend the pressures generated by society's arrangement of power;

and these are values that do not tend to excite critical analysis of those very arrangements.

Conclusion

From our historical distance the pathos of this "innocent theorizing" is easy to spot. It would be anachronistically unfair to belabor Newman for it. But such "innocent theorizing" does caution us regarding current reflections on the idea of theological education. Proposals about what makes theological education theological dare not pretend to independence of persons' social location and institutions' interest. If, following Newman, it is suggested (1) that the unity of a theological school's education lies in the end to which it is ordered, (2) that this end is pursued for its own sake and not for any further practical consequences, (3) that precisely for that reason it gives the theological school a public calling and mission, and (4) that this view does justice to the pluralism characterizing theological schools, how shall we avoid the abstractness and ideological bias illustrated by Newman's lectures? Our analysis of these difficulties with Newman's arguments suggests that the answer lies in large part in careful attention to assumptions about human nature. A commitment to keep the discussion of theological schools as concrete as possible, passing through their concrete pluralism rather than transcendentally flying over them by way of abstractions, must be accompanied by a view of human nature that honors the social concreteness of human persons.

Paideia and Excellence in Theological Schooling

Paideia is an unavoidable model of excellence for theological schools today in North America. We have seen that this is true for historical reasons. Christianity has been pictured as a kind of

47

paideia for so long that the picture is firmly grounded in the deepest level that an archaeological dig can reach. Simply to characterize a school as a "Christian" theological school is to invoke this picture. This is true despite the fact, as we shall see in the next chapter, that paideia has until recently never been explicitly lifted up as the model of excellent schooling in North American studies that explore what theological schools are and should be.

Granted that, it will be well to keep in mind these major cautionary lessons to be learned from our review of the lineaments of the "Athens" type in its modern form:

- that it is a particularly powerful model by which to analyze theological education basically, not in terms of its curriculum nor in terms of the dynamics of its educational processes, but in terms of its overarching goal or purpose;
- that it is particularly illuminating to analyze specifically Christian theological education, not in terms of the over-arching purpose of conveying information or well-warranted truths to students, but in terms of helping them become formed (or in-formed) by certain dispositions to act in certain ways (including actions associated with thought and speech);
- that this makes it particularly important to be attentive to the view of human personhood whose validity is assumed by various proposals about how to understand theological education;
- and, finally, that it is especially important to employ views of human personhood and of institutions such as schools that do not inappropriately abstract them from the factors that help make them the concretely particular realities they are, including such factors as their historical, cultural, social, and economic locations.

3

"Berlin" in Early
Twentieth-Century America

The "Berlin" type of excellent theological education, which comprises the two distinct enterprises of *Wissenschaft* and "professional" education for ministry, came to dominate Protestant theological education in North America by the middle of the twentieth century, in large part in the wake of a series of major studies of theological education that were widely read and sometimes led to significant reforms. It is important to see the current debate over what is "theological" about theological education in the context of this longer intellectual history of reflection on theological schooling. The studies in question introduced material modifications into the "Berlin" type, and the modifications in turn have led to serious incoherences in widely accepted pictures of what theological education ought to be. Much of the current debate can be read as an effort to correct those incoherences. In order to see exactly what is at issue in the current debate, therefore, it will be important to be as clear as possible about the modifications of the "Berlin" type that appear to have led to problems now needing correction.

The modifications of the "Berlin" type, and the incoherences in theological education to which they seem to have led, come at four points. The "professional" education pole of the model has been reconceived. Where Schleiermacher had proposed a field of "practical theology" that identified the normative rules governing authentically Christian practices, especially ministerial practices, in a communal or ecclesial way, "practical theology" has now come to be conceived as training individuals to perform a heterogeneous set of ministerial functions. "Professional" education for ministerial leadership has been reconceived in a functionalist and individualistic way.

Correlatively, the array of forms of *Wissenschaft* that theological education embraces has been dramatically expanded. Where Schleiermacher had stressed historical and philosophical research, a much larger number of the social and human sciences have now been added. Far too many of them are included for students to be able to learn how to *do* any of them for themselves. One result of this is that the *wissenschaftlich* pole of theological education has become more an exercise in communicating to students the results of critical inquiry than an exercise teaching them to engage in critical inquiry themselves.

Third, the relation between *Wissenschaft* and "professional" education has been reconceived. Schleiermacher had proposed that educating people to engage in relevant critical inquiry could provide a foundation for their engaging in practical theology. The modifications in the two poles of the "Berlin" type, however, have left the relation between them much more vague. It is no longer clear what the movement is in theological education from critical inquiry to practical theology, from *Wissenschaft* to "professional" education for church leadership.

Finally, with one very important exception, these influential studies of theological education have not themselves been exercises in theological reflection. Neither the reasons given for making these modifications of the "Berlin" type nor the analysis of problems that seemed to require these modifications has taken the form of theological reflection. Mostly they have been prudential and pragmatic reflections.

W. R. Harper

In retrospect, W. R. Harper's 1899 manifesto "Shall the Theological Curriculum Be Modified and How" was the harbinger of these changes in the "Berlin" type.[1] When the University of Chicago was founded, a divinity school was deliberately located at its geographic and, hopefully, intellectual center. Thus, a theological school had been included in a university that was self-consciously defined as a research university. Harper, the university's first president, intended his new theological school to be at once scholarly and professional in a way that could "meet the requirements of modern times." To accomplish this the conventional curriculum of theological schools would need to be modified according to two principles: first, the curriculum should be modified to "accord with the assured results of modern psychology and pedagogy, as well as with the demands which have been made apparent by our common experience" (46); and second, the curriculum should be modified "to meet the demands suggested by the character of the field in which the student is to work . . . in other words . . . the present state of society" (48).

On the scholarly side these two principles suggested several

1. Harper, "Shall the Theological Curriculum Be Modified and How," *The American Journal of Theology* 3, 1 (Jan. 1899): 45-66; subsequent citations will be made parenthetically in the text.

things to Harper. A theological school ought to be "organized in connection with a university" (66). It ought to employ pedagogical methods characteristic of the research university, such as research seminars and freedom to elect courses ("freedom to learn/freedom to teach").[2] Harper agrees with Schleiermacher's view that Scripture ought to be critically taught, always in its historical context, perhaps thereby accepting the view that biblical studies comprise one more subsection of "historical theology" (54). On the other hand, Harper's major thesis regarding critical inquiry in a theological school is that it must bring the student "into touch with the modern spirit of science" (49). By this Harper means not merely the spirit of critical inquiry generally but specifically "modern psychology" (which he says "is as yet largely unknown" in theological schools), and even actual laboratory work in the physical sciences (53). In the midst of this theology forms the organizing center. Thus, already at the turn of the century an influential theological educator is calling for considerable pluralization of the sorts of critical inquiry a theological school is to embrace.

On the professional side Harper's two principles suggested the following: "The day has come for a broadening of the meaning of the word minister, and for the cultivation of specialism in the ministry, as well as in medicine, in law, and in teaching" (59). Harper lists as distinct "specialisms" — each of which should have its own curricular track — preaching, pastoral work, teaching, administration, medicine (on analogy with medical missionaries), and music (56-59). Each of these requires practical training in "theological clinics" and in supervised field experience (61-62). Here it is already taken for granted that "professional" practice is to be understood in a functionalist way, and that the bodies of theory that must inform this practice

2. Cf. Harper, pp. 61 and 59.

come from the human sciences and not from Schleiermacher's "philosophical theology."

Harper's essay reflects the energetic optimism of the best of turn-of-the-century progressivism. It celebrates not only American society's "spirit of science" but also its "democratic spirit," confident that the combination of scientific research and democratic methods could overcome any problems — in this case the possibility that "mainline" Protestantism might lose its cultural hegemony in American society. Harper is quite open that that is his central interest:

> The condition of the churches, both rural and urban, is not upon the whole encouraging. Ministers of the better class are not satisfied to accept the rural churches; and yet these same ministers are not strong enough, or sufficiently prepared, to meet the demands of many city churches. (45)

His naive use of class differences to identify excellence ("Ministers of the better class are not satisfied to accept the rural churches") and his explicit call for theological schools to train persons to minister specifically to the rich (cf. 49) suggest that this interest in theology, which is otherwise so thoroughly underemployed in Harper's proposed reform of theological schooling, is vulnerable to ideological misuse as a "cover" that at once obscures and legitimates an underlying concern to secure the churches' social status.

Harper's essay may not itself have had much direct impact on American theological schools apart from the University of Chicago Divinity School, but his essay does symbolize modifications in Schleiermacher's picture of a professional school within a research university that were considerably developed in a later series of major studies of theological education, studies which did have great impact on theological schools through the next half century. Comparison of these studies brings into relief subtle but historically influential shifts in the meaning of "professional" (as in "theological schools are professional schools"), in the sorts of research deemed important to "professional" ministry, and in the ways in which research functions in professional schooling.

Robert L. Kelly and William Adams Brown

The first two of these studies were published roughly a decade apart: Robert L. Kelly's *Theological Education in America* in 1924 and William Adams Brown and Mark A. May's four-volume study *The Education of American Ministers* in 1935.[3] A major purpose of both studies was fact-finding. They collected and published otherwise unavailable comparative information about Protestant theological schools' student bodies, including their educational backgrounds, programs of study, finances, and governance, and also about these schools' faculty, including their educational backgrounds, teaching methods, religious life, etc. However, each study was also charged with recommending changes based on the information gathered. It is the character of these studies' recommendations — and, just as revealing, the sorts of arguments made in support of the recommendations — that exhibit the changing shape of the "Berlin" model of excellence for theological schooling.

One overriding plea was made by both studies — namely, that theological schooling needs to have more rigorous academic standards appropriate to a much more clearly defined professional education. "It is a fair question," Kelly dryly observed, "whether the seminaries, as a group of schools, are centers of intellectual

---

3. Kelly, *Theological Education in America* (New York: George H. Doran Co., 1924); Brown and May, *The Education of American Ministers*, 4 vols. (New York: The Institute of Social and Religious Research, 1934).

and ethical power."[4] "Many seminaries," he pointed out, "could scarcely qualify as educational institutions since they neither speak the language nor use the methods of modern education" (228). Warning the seminaries against complacency, he points out that "the churches are demanding many new types of workers" who, he seems to suggest, may well be supplied not by the seminaries but by "Bible schools and religious training schools," the "recent growth" of which means that they "now enroll as many students as all the seminaries" (229). Similarly, Brown begins his reflections on the implications of his study's fact-finding by pointing to one statistic with alarm:

> An analysis of the 1926 Religious Census figures for seventeen of the largest white Protestant denominations in the United States, shows that two out of five of all the ministers of these denominations were graduates neither of college nor of theological seminary, while only one in three was a graduate of both. One need not exaggerate the importance of purely academic training in a profession in which personal qualities count for so much as in the ministry to feel that a situation like this must cause serious concern.[5]

Kelly's principal recommendation toward correcting this situation (and fending off the competition of the "Bible schools and religious training schools"?) is that theological schools accept common standards. That will involve formulating accepted "definitions of various types of institutions and of phases of work. . . . The definition, as a working hypothesis, is a most efficient means

---

4. Kelly, p. 236; subsequent citations will be made parenthetically in the text.

5. Brown, *Ministerial Education in America*, vol. 1 of Brown and May's *Education of American Ministers*, p. 4; subsequent citations will be made parenthetically in the text.

of educational advancement; sound definitions set forth attainable educational goals" (Kelly, 220).

Brown repeatedly celebrates the advantages of theological schooling that is academically rigorous.[6] Perhaps going beyond Kelly, he seems implicitly to urge that one of the standards should be that theological schooling is by definition graduate schooling, presupposing that its students have already completed an under-graduate degree. Following up on Kelly's plea that the standards and definitions of excellence in theological education "be agreed upon by the seminaries themselves, working not as now largely in isolation but in cooperation with other educational agencies" (Kelly, 220), Brown urged a decade after Kelly that a "Council of Seminaries" be formed, among the responsibilities of which would be the formulating and policing of standards (cf. Brown, 222-26).

The historical influence of these two studies has resulted in the formation of just such a council. Over time it has developed into the present Association of Theological Schools. The creature of the theological schools themselves, it is above all their accrediting agency. It is the vehicle by which they are able to do what Kelly said was needed: define themselves and police their adherence to their own standards of excellence in schooling.

The historical importance of these two studies is not limited to their generating a sense of urgency about the founding of such a council, however. Beyond that, they legitimated a particular model of excellence in theological schooling that deeply formed the ethos of the world of theological schools. It is something like a background conventional wisdom shaping debates about standards for theological schooling. It is a modification of the picture of excellent theological schooling rooted in Schleiermacher's rationale for a school of theology in the University of Berlin. The

6. Cf. Brown, chap. 3.

modifications they legitimated have been fateful. We can see this by looking closely at what Kelly and Brown mean by "professional" and how they relate their understanding of "professional" to critical, orderly, disciplined inquiry.

In both studies "professional" seems principally to connote "esteem" and "competence." Infusing both of these meanings is a background anxiety that the education of Protestant ministers has not kept up with radical developments in knowledge nor with changes in educational standards and procedures in the twentieth century, and thus that the ministry may not "hold its own with the leaders of the other professions" (Brown, 4) and might slip from its traditional parity in esteem with law and medicine. Esteem, it seems to be supposed, follows from competence.

But competence in what? It is remarkable that neither study contains any sustained theological reflection on that question. Both studies simply proceed from this basic assumption: theological schools are defined by the task of educating ministers for the churches. Accordingly, if we want to know what the relevant competencies are for the ministry, we must ask the churches what they expect in their ministers.[7]

Here, in company with W. R. Harper, Kelly and Brown depart from Schleiermacher's understanding of "professional." Schleiermacher had defined law, medicine, and ministry as "professions" by reference to the leadership each gives to practices that are indispensable to the well-being of *society* as a whole. With regard to Protestant Christian ministry, that might make sense when Protestant Christianity is the nation's established religion; but in twentieth-century America it is not. The practices for which religious leadership needs to have competencies can therefore only be specified by the average expressed expectations of the individual persons who voluntarily assemble to form a church. Approached in

---

7. Cf. Kelly, pp. 61, 210; Brown, p. 74, chap. 2 passim.

this way, the competencies required by ministry are defined not theologically but functionally. They are defined by the roles church members expect their ministers to play in their lives.

This is largely implicit in Kelly's assumptions and method (but cf. Kelly, 223). It is explicit in Brown. Brown identifies five such roles — teacher, preacher/evangelist, worship leader, pastor, and administrator (Brown, 21) — and acknowledges the necessity for specialization in one of them (60). However, in contrast to Harper, he is dubious about the wisdom of requiring students to specialize early in their education (61). Brown sharpens the functionalism of this view of "professional" by the utilitarian criteria he adopts to measure competence: "efficiency," "esteem," and "success" in ministry.

Here the character of Brown's argument that theological schools ought to adopt higher academic standards is particularly revealing. It is precisely measures of efficiency, success, and local esteem — that is, measures of competence in fulfilling certain functions in persons' lives — that prove the importance of academically demanding theological schooling:

> Judged by all these measures of testing, the result seems conclusive. In terms of the size of the church, those men who have had both a college and a seminary training provide a ministry which is from 40 to 75 per cent. more effective than that furnished by ministers who have had neither. The internal organization of churches served by such ministers proves on the whole superior to that of churches manned by untrained ministers. While the results reached by a study of the minister's social activities and community service leads to the same conclusion. (55)

Higher standards of academic work in theological schooling pay off in ministry. The argument for high academic standards appeals to practical utility, not to theological considerations concerning ministry.

Accordingly, both Kelly and Brown recommend the introduction into theological schools of types of schooling that will directly develop those skills that students need in order to fulfill the functions of ministry. They call for increased use of case study teaching methods and of the practicum, for more attention to pressing social issues, for more deliberate globalization of the context of teaching, and for more care to teach students and not simply to teach subject matters.[8]

At the same time they both clearly call for increased stress on *Wissenschaft* in theological schooling. What is less clear is how this is understood to be related to the schooling in applicable skills that is required by their functionalist understanding of "professional"; thus the farther their approach in excellence is followed, the deeper theological schools are driven into internal incoherence and fragmentation. The call for increase of *Wissenschaft* is clear in Kelly. He laments that "there are evidences that goodness rather than intelligence is often held up as an end of theological teaching" and that "with rare exceptions the seminaries are not conspicuous as centers of scholarly pursuits" (Kelly, 235). He characterizes research as the " 'nervous system of the university' stimulating every part of it," and he calls for seminaries to become "repositories of the latest and most accurate data upon which educational, social and industrial as well as religious programs for the present day may be based" (222-23). Kelly notes that only a few theological schools "make the claim that their institutions are committed to the scientific procedure" (215). Raising no objection to the already fragmented curriculum, Kelly implicitly urges that, in addition to all of the various existing disciplines, others be added from the social and psychological sciences. Moreover, he calls explicitly for the inclusion of laboratory sciences (229).

8. Cf. Kelly, pp. 215-30; Brown, pp. 59-62, 95-98, 183-217.

Not only is no thought given to how to unify all of this into a single coherent course of study, but no attention is given to how anything more than a rudimentary introduction can be given to so many different research disciplines. What is called for in the classroom here is not research but reports of research done elsewhere. It is difficult to see how teaching in this context could really be an exercise in the shared research that should characterize teaching and learning according to the "Berlin" model. Perhaps Kelly's one comment about this is his suggestion that theological schooling find "a method of popularizing . . . without resorting to the sensational" (227). The suggestion would have appalled Schleiermacher.

Brown stresses excellence in the "classical academic" areas far more than does Kelly. It is not clear, however, whether Brown's constant stress on high academic expectations simply assumes the canons of critical, orderly, disciplined inquiry that the research university model had made commonplace in the 1930s in American graduate education outside of theological schools, or whether he is rather calling for theological school teachers who are very learned but are not necessarily themselves engaged in original research.

Brown focuses far more than Kelly does on the structure and unity of a theological school's curriculum. He seems to think that the problem of fragmentation in the course of study can be overcome with relative ease. According to Brown, underlying the diversity of academic disciplines is a set of "basic philosophical and historical questions which constitute the presupposition of all effective ministerial work" (Brown, 61). He organizes these questions using a version of Schleiermacher's threefold curricular structure, dividing this structure into what he calls three "fields": historical studies (including study of the Bible), interpretation of Christianity (including theological, sociological, and psychological interpretations), and "the work of Christianity in the present"

(122). These "fields" are not just academic "disciplines," nor are they exclusively research specializations. They include several disciplines and specializations (128). Brown calls for more cross-disciplinary teaching and thinks that this structure of fields will make that easier to do (140). To help further overcome fragmentation of the course of study, he proposes that some new way of measuring movement through the course of study be adopted to replace the "semester hour" or "term hour," which tends to atomize the curriculum. Perhaps, he suggests, student achievement can be measured by way of comprehensive examinations or by reference to what is expected of the student (130).

It may be that Brown can be so sanguine about overcoming the fragmenting effects of disciplinary diversity because the national scholarly organizations that institutionalize the various academic guilds today exercised less political power in the 1930s over scholars' standing with peers, mobility from school to school, and promotion to tenure. In any case it is striking that this proposal lacks any rationale that determines which disciplines ought to be included within the course of study based on a *theological* understanding of the nature and purpose of the church, the nature of ministry, or even the nature of theology itself broadly construed. Instead, the proposal appears simply to rearrange pieces inherited from the tradition according to the various ways in which they bear on students' acquiring the level of skill they need in order to fulfill the functions of ministry with "professional" competence. As with Kelly's recommendations, the rhetoric of this proposal honors *Wissenschaft* in theological schooling, but the proposal's structure gives schooling in critical, systematic, disciplined inquiry no role to play in the "training" of religious "professionals."

This widening gap between critical inquiry and "professional training" of clergy makes more acute the constant threat of ideological captivity of theological schooling. (Kelly is unusual in warning theological schools of this danger; see Kelly, 230.) There are, of course, no structures or procedures that can be devised to guarantee that a school's interest in its social and cultural privileges will not bias its education, legitimate those privileges religiously, and then subtly but systematically obscure the bias.

One possible check on this tendency is rigorous critical examination of the forms of speech and action in which the school is training its students. But even that possibility of ideology critique is weakened when education in critical inquiry is effectively disassociated from education in "professional" roles and functions. Their uncritical acceptance of a functionalist and individualistic picture of "professional" ministry leaves both Kelly and Brown vulnerable on this point. The "functions" for which theological schools are to prepare future clergy are determined by the expectations of the membership of "mainline" white Protestant churches, and in general that membership expects ministerial leadership to be "successful" and "efficient" (Brown, 55) in helping them to preserve their social status and cultural roles in a nation that is entering a future marked by unprecedented urbanization, technological change, and massive social planning (Kelly, 230-31).

The insistence that theological education must keep students in touch with current intellectual and cultural developments is, of course, Kelly's and Brown's recapitulation of the "Berlin" model's contention that excellent education must engage the public world. As we have noted, the possibility that clergy might fail to develop these skills is reflected in fears that poorly schooled ministers will slip from their social parity with lawyers and physicians and become indistinguishable from graduates of Bible colleges. By the same token, the quality of theological schools is to be measured by the degree to which they are capable of keeping their students in touch with those changes. Brown, for example, is confident that "progress" in theological schooling will come through the national influence of a few elite schools (cf. Brown, 5). "Elite" status for both Brown and Kelly correlates with a school's uncritical appropriation of the nation's "democratic spirit" (cf. Kelly, 231), with its confidence in social progress (largely through education), technological advances, and skillful management. Elite theological schools would be able to "train" their students to fulfill their functions as ministers in just that spirit. Whatever the role of *Wissenschaft* might be in such schools, it would certainly be in no position to call that "spirit" into question.[9]

The legacy that these two enormously influential studies left to theological education in North America, then, has been thoroughly ambiguous. They effectively urged that theological education should have more rigorous academic standards appropriate to much more highly defined professional education. They framed their recommendations in the conventions of Schleiermacher's rationale for the inclusion of theology as a "professional school" within the University of Berlin and thereby brought every theological school under the standards of that model. However, at the same time they legitimated a functionalist modification of the professional school model. That led to bifurcation of the model: Kelly and Brown urged *both* critical inquiry of a high order *and* training in "professional" roles and skills, but they could show no integral relation between the two. Furthermore, they called for a great increase in the sorts of critical inquiry that are relevant, especially from the human sciences. The sheer number of types of critical inquiry guaranteed, on the *Wissenschaft* side, that no student could be taught to *do* any of them, which is precisely what the research university model calls for. And the sheer number of roles

---

9. It gives pause to recall that Reinhold Niebuhr, who would later bring precisely that "spirit" into question, was already teaching on William Adams Brown's faculty at Union Theological Seminary when the Brown-May study was published in 1935!

and functions deemed to constitute "ministry" guaranteed, on the professional side, that no student could be schooled to apply the inquiry to cases on his or her own. The obvious question is whether schooling on this modified "Berlin" model can educate either "pure" or "applied" theological inquirers.

That creates a great irony. Although it celebrates the sense of "rationality" associated with the Enlightenment and institutionalized by the research university, such theological schooling would not in fact cultivate that rationality in its students! Moreover, the functions for which students are to be prepared are largely socially defined and are divorced from critical inquiry that might help to check ideological captivity of accepted ministerial functions. Under the impact of this modification of the "Berlin" model, theological schooling tends to undergo a movement from pure academic research to applied academic research (both done at the hands of academic theologians) to popularization of the applied research (by theological school teachers) to repetitions of the popularizations by practitioners (the students).

H. Richard Niebuhr, Daniel Day Williams, and James M. Gustafson

The third and most recent major comprehensive study of Protestant theological schools, published in 1956 and 1957, was undertaken by the American Association of Theological Schools (now simply the Association of Theological Schools), funded by the Carnegie Foundation, and directed by H. Richard Niebuhr, Daniel Day Williams, and James M. Gustafson. The study was published in two volumes: *The Purpose of the Church and Its Ministry,* in which Niebuhr developed a theological account of ministry on the basis of a theological analysis of what the church is, and a report and interpretation of research prepared by the three investigators, *The Advancement of Theological Education*.[10]

Implicitly the study moves to counter the three sorts of change in Schleiermacher's model of a *wissenschaftlich* "professional" school that we found in the Kelly and May-Brown studies: the abandonment of a specifically theological account of the subject matter of the *Wissenschaft;* the individualistic and functionalist understanding of "professional"; and a separation of *Wissenschaft* from professional training that leaves both incapable of internal critique of ideological differences.

It is, of course, important in noting the striking differences between the findings of this study and those of its predecessors to recall the enormous social and cultural changes that had taken place in the intervening twenty years. At the time of the May-Brown study there had been serious economic depression. The intervening years had seen World War II; the rise of the United States to "superpower" status as (in its own view) the guarantor of the security of the "free world," a status underwritten by nuclear power and illustrated by the United States' participation in a United Nations "police action" in Korea; and rapid economic growth and high prosperity. In addition, something like a religious revival seemed to be taking place, and the churches were fuller than they had been for decades.[11] The study found that in general

> there were four times as many genuinely graduate schools of theology in the United States and Canada in 1955 as there were in 1923 [the time of the Kelly study] and that such schools enroll almost eight times as many students as they did thirty-two years

10. Niebuhr, *The Purpose of the Church and Its Ministry* (New York: Harper & Row, 1956); Niebuhr, Williams, and Gustafson, *The Advancement of Theological Education* (New York: Harper & Row, 1957).

11. Cf. Will Herberg, *Protestant, Catholic, Jew: An Essay in American Religious Sociology* (Garden City, NY: Doubleday, 1955).

previously. Most of this increase in graduate work in theology has taken place since the time of the publication of the May-Brown report.[12]

Absent now are the worries that graduate (i.e., post-baccalaureate) theological schools will fail to attract enough able students to meet the needs of increasingly urbanized and sophisticated churches: "While the increase in theological enrollment has not kept up with the increases in graduate school or college enrollment, nevertheless it has exceeded the rate of growth recorded in Protestant church membership" (11). Indeed, now the perceived problem in this regard is the need for an "institutionalization and refinement of admissions procedures" (183), coupled with a need to be skeptically cautious about the usefulness of psychological testing instruments (181), in the interest of selecting the most qualified and promising students and sparing the others frustration and wasted resources.

Absent too are the worries that graduate theological schooling on the "Berlin" model of excellence might be overwhelmed by schooling on the non-*wissenschaftlich* model symbolized by Bible schools: "The evidence is that not less than 80 percent of the estimated total enrollment of theological students in the United States and Canada consists of college graduates," compared with Brown and May's finding in 1924 that only "44 per cent of seminary students had college degrees" (8-9).

Another sign of the flourishing of graduate professional theological schools was the discovery that about half of all such schools "had undertaken new construction or major renovation during the decade since the end of World War II" (27). The study points out that "conspicuous" among this building was an "interest in library improvement," but it laments "the lack in school after school of

12. Niebuhr, Williams, and Gustafson, p. 8; subsequent citations will be made parenthetically in the text.

sufficient seminar rooms, and, perhaps even more, . . . the failure of many schools to feel pressure at this point" (28). It is as though the resources needed to support the research called for by *Wissenschaft* were being attended to, but the resources needed for the peculiar sort of teaching and learning that *Wissenschaft* calls for were being ignored. Yet another sign of the flourishing of AATS-member graduate professional schools in the United States was the astonishing — from the vantage of the 1990s — statistic that despite the intervening economic depression they averaged three times as much endowment per student ($6,103) as all privately controlled academic institutions ($2,040), and more than ten times as much as publicly controlled institutions ($455).[13]

The Course of Study

In the study's view, the central problems confronting theological schools in the mid-1950s had to do, not with students or resources or commitment to high academic standards, but with the course of study. Here it saw four problems: uncertainty about the ultimate "goal or end of theological education . . . , the overloading of the curriculum, the extension of requirements, and the loss of unity among so many specialized courses" (80). These problems resulted from two historical developments. On the one hand, theological schools have done precisely what the Kelly and May-Brown studies, and Harper before them, had urged. They have added course work in "nontheological" disciplines, especially psychology and sociology, and field-based "learning by doing" courses (cf. 21-22). On the other hand, "emphasis on the importance of the traditional disciplines of theological study in the biblical, church-historical and systematic fields has been reinforced after a period in which their values were frequently ques-

13. Niebuhr, Williams, and Gustafson, p. 33.

tioned" (21). Curricular overload was inevitable, and so was the consequent tendency to guarantee that every student be exposed to all of it by extending course requirements.

The authors of this study focus on the problem of the loss of unity in the course of study. For resolution of the problem they look, not to the recovery of a single subject matter whose inherent structure could unify a course of study, but rather to reformed teaching and differently trained faculty. In their final chapter, "The Line of Advance," they find that

> the greatest defect in theological education today is that it is too much an affair of piecemeal transmission of knowledge and skills, and that, in consequence, it offers too little challenge to the student to develop his own resources and to become an independent, lifelong inquirer, growing constantly while he is engaged in the work of the ministry. (209; emphasis omitted)

Hence they conclude "that the key problem in theological education in the Protestantism of the United States and Canada is that of providing and maintaining the most able corps of teaching theologians and theological teachers possible" (203).

The study's firm adherence to the "Berlin" model is especially clear here. By helping students to become self-educating, excellent teaching prepares them for ministry: the clergy paradigm for professional theological schooling is taken for granted. However, good teaching does not accomplish this by concentrating on "vocational training" in ministerial "needs and skills" (111): functionalist understandings of the profession are rejected. Rather, good teaching helps students to become self-educating by the traditional methods of *Wissenschaft:* "objective analysis, discovery, and interpretation" of various topics (144).

The study gives an eloquent picture of the "good teacher" on the "Berlin" model of excellence in theological schooling. Teaching needs to be reformed because too much of it is didactic, ingrown, and piecemeal. When "an inert mass of fact and idea . . . is handed in small pieces by the teacher to the student then the heart of intellectual inquiry is betrayed" (134). Instead of this didactic approach, excellent teaching calls for students and teachers together to work on subject matter so concentratedly that "the student sees the professor's mind at work on a problem, grappling with its difficulties and seeking more light" (141), and through their joint venture learns how to engage in this sort of study for himself or herself. Echoes of Humboldt can be clearly distinguished here. Moreover, in its examination of problems of government in theological schools (chap. 3), the study continues in the tradition of the University of Berlin by voicing a powerful protest against patterns of school governance that "seem to have little confidence in the power of God to establish the victory of truth" (44) and an eloquent plea for the freedom of inquiry that disciplined critical inquiry requires.

Second, theological teaching is ingrown when it fails to "enter into a dialogue with contemporary thought and culture" (87). It is assumed without question that the traditional fourfold theological curriculum of Bible, history, systematic theology, and practical theology will be part of the subject matter to be studied.[14] But like the Kelly and May-Brown studies, this study also insists that philosophy, psychology, and sociology "are essential to the full understanding of the Christian faith itself" (87). Indeed, it emphatically insists

> that no theological faculty is complete until it includes some [scholars] who share the Christian outlook and faith and who are competent to explore scientific and cultural problems with the same rigor with which secular experts in those fields are trained. (65)

14. Cf. Niebuhr, Williams, and Gustafson, chap. 5, "The Course of Study," esp. pp. 78-90.

Presumably because such changes help to meet this need, the study seems to approve the tendency it sees in theological schools to move toward closer affiliations with universities (cf. 52). "Professional" education for ministry must be conducted in the context of *wissenschaftlich* research.

Finally, theological teaching needs to be reformed when it has become piecemeal. It becomes piecemeal, the study holds, because it is done so individualistically. The remedy lies in increased collegiality and cooperation among the various specializations making up a faculty. The study does see a "general tendency . . . toward a greater emphasis on cooperation and the achievement of a genuine community within the faculty," and it calls for the development of ways to further this trend (67). The picture of good teaching developed here to counter the fragmentation of theological schooling also tends to counter the previous two studies' tendency to change the "Berlin" model of theological schooling by adopting a functionalist picture of "professional" schooling and an individualistic picture of the teaching proper to *Wissenschaft*.

Suitably reformed theological teaching will be able to hold together schooling in critical, disciplined research and schooling for professional ministry, but only indirectly. Nothing about the rigors of *Wissenschaft* logically implies the capacities for professional ministry. Nor, contrary to the "essence hunt," is there some essential structure to theological knowledge that will unify theological schooling. To be sure, there are interconnections among the topics in the curriculum that must be traced (cf. 82-83). And the study does endorse a modified core curriculum (cf. 84). Nonetheless, unity in theological schooling finally lies not in its structure but in *how* it is done, the *manner* in which it is undertaken (cf. 201).

Good theological teaching will therefore engage in "objective analysis, discovery, and interpretation" (144), but always in the context of the Christian faith, so that the students discover that their own personal commitments are bound up with what they are studying (cf. 141). It will not only "continually be pushing students to examine the ultimate presuppositions with which they think" (142) but will also keep a close relationship "between the formal structure of thought and concrete human problems" (143) and between the subject matter and students' vocational commitments. Finally, however, doing theological teaching in this manner rests on an act of faith:

> It is difficult to say precisely how it is that our relationship to God can be the central theme of theological teaching while the process remains that of objective analysis, discovery, and interpretation. But such is the case when the teacher knows what he is about, for the most effective work is done by those who keep this ultimate dimension of their subject clear. (144)

This brings us to the point at which this study differs decisively from previous studies of Protestant theological education. The authors of *The Advancement of Theological Education* are not so naive as to suppose that the fragmented theological course of study can be unified simply by increasing faculty collegiality. There is a deeper reason for fragmentation than simply American individualism, and that reason is a theological one in the strictest sense, an issue about God and about faithlessness to God. The underlying reason for the fragmentation of theological schooling is deep confusion of proximate with ultimate goals, a confusion of functional idolatry with radical faith, the remedy for which must be a kind of repentance. H. Richard Niebuhr explored this confusion in the first volume of the study, *The Purpose of the Church and Its Ministry*.

Accepting the "Berlin" model's understanding of a theological school as a "graduate professional school," Niebuhr pursues a basically simple line of questioning in *The Purpose of the Church*

and Its Ministry. He begins by asserting that what makes a professional school "professional" is its task of preparing religious
leaders, ministers. But what is ministry? There is a great deal of
confusion about that. Accepting with Schleiermacher that a professional school exists to prepare an "indispensable leadership,"
Niebuhr assumes with Kelly and Brown that this is a leadership
indispensable to the church but not, as Schleiermacher had it, to
society as a whole. That is, the nature of ministry must be defined,
not by an account of society's needs, but by an account of the
purposes of the church. And there is a great deal of confusion
about that. Clarity about the nature of theological schooling
depends on clarity about the nature of ministry; and clarity about
ministry depends on clarity about the purpose of the church. And
that is a theological question.

The basic question is how to understand God and God's
relation to the church and its ministry. Thus the doctrine of God
is the subtext of Niebuhr's book. The view of God that emerges
in this book might be fittingly described as "radical prophetic
monotheism."[15] God is the One beyond the many, "the Source
and Center of all being, the Determiner of destiny, the Universal
One" on whom we are "completely, absolutely dependent; who
is the Mystery behind the mystery of human existence . . . , the
One from whom death proceeds as well as life . . . who appears
as God of wrath as well as God of love."[16] It is "apparently
necessary" to understand this One in Trinitarian terms (21). What
makes this monotheism "radical" is its insistence that God is
beyond *all* the many, including the "many" through whom we
apprehend God: Scripture, church, even Jesus Christ himself. As

15. The allusion, of course, is to Niebuhr's *Radical Monotheism and Western
Culture* (New York: Harper & Row, 1960), which provides the larger framework
within which *The Purpose of the Church and Its Ministry* is best understood.

16. Niebuhr, *The Purpose of the Church and Its Ministry,* pp. 36-37; subsequent citations will be made parenthetically in the text.

the ground of our being and value, God alone is the proper Object of our ultimate loyalty and love. In actual practice we constantly confuse this ultimate Object of our loyalty and love with more proximate and relative objects. This monotheism is "prophetically" radical, then, in seeing God's presence as a call to constant repentance and conversion from this idolatrous confusion of proximate and ultimate.

The church must be defined only by reference to God: "By Church, first of all, we mean the subjective pole of the objective rule of God. . . . It is the subject that apprehends its Object; that thinks the Other; worships and depends on It; imitates It perhaps; sometimes reflects It; but is always distinct from its Object" (19). The "subject" is marked by several polarities: it is at once community and institution, one and many, local and universal, protestant and catholic (i.e., finite "incarnation" of the infinite), and finds itself constantly in polarity with the world that is its companion before God (cf. 21-27). However, the church's purpose is not defined by any of these, neither by community building nor by maintenance of institution, neither by promotion of denominational programs nor by world-inclusive mission, neither by prophetic action nor by symbolizing the holy in space and time, neither by protecting itself from the world nor by serving the world. Rather, the purpose of the church must be defined by reference to God: "the goal of the Church [is] the *increase among men [and women] of the love of God and neighbor*" (31). Confusion and conflict within the church concerning the church's nature are intensified and even generated by substitution of proximate goals for this ultimate one.

More to our point, theological education is self-contradictory when it confuses "church, considered as a whole or in its essence, with the ultimate context of theological education" (41).

When it prevails such education necessarily becomes indoctrination in Christian principles rather than inquiry based on faith in

God; or it is turned into training in methods for increasing the Church rather than for guiding men to love of God and neighbor.

So too, theological schooling is thrown into self-contradiction "when the Bible is so made the center of theological education that the book takes the place of the God who speaks" (43). Above all, "the most prevalent, the most deceptive and perhaps ultimately the most dangerous inconsistency to which churches and schools are subject . . . arises from the substitution of Christology for theology, of the love of Jesus Christ for the love of God" (44).

Niebuhr makes this point on the basis of his own emphatic christocentrism. The church may not be the only community directed toward God, but

its uniqueness lies in its particular relation to that reality, a relation inseparable from Jesus Christ . . . in the sense that Jesus Christ is the center of this community directed toward God; the Church takes its stand with Jesus Christ before God and knows him, though with many limitations, with the mind of Christ. (20)

Nonetheless, that which is known only through and inseparably from Jesus Christ is precisely the One beyond the many, who ought not to be confused even with Jesus Christ. When that confusion does happen "the faith of Christians is converted into a Christian religion for which Jesus Christ in isolation is the one object of devotion" (45). In order for theological education to overcome its self-contradictions and recover unity it needs to repent its placing ultimate love and loyalty in these proximate purposes and convert to placing all its proximate goals within the context of faith in the One beyond the many.

Given this view of the purpose of the church, what is the purpose of its ministry? There is a good deal of confusion in the church about the nature of the ministry and therefore a good bit

74

of confusion in theological schools' pictures of what sort of leadership they are preparing. There are, of course, a number of activities involved in ministry: preaching, teaching, pastoral care, leading worship, management, etc. And these activities have been directed to various proximate goals: saving souls, curing guilty souls, reconciling estranged souls through sacraments, etc. Coherent pictures of the ministry have emerged in the past when one of the activities was selected as most important and was aimed at one proximate goal, while all the other activities were directed to that same goal, in subordination to the most important activity. Thus, for example, for Gregory the Great the most important activity was the pastoral government of souls, aimed at helping them to avoid sin and to attain everlasting life; all other ministerial activities — such as preaching, celebrating the sacraments, and church administration — were directed toward that same goal in subordination to pastoral governance. "If there is confusion in the conception of the ministry today," Niebuhr declared, "that confusion appears at both points — in inability to define what the most important activity of the ministry is and in uncertainty about the proximate end toward which all its activities are directed" (63).

Despite this confusion, Niebuhr claimed that there was "an emerging new conception of the ministry" in the churches (57). "For want of a better phrase we may name it the conception of the minister as a pastoral director, though the name is of little importance" (80). The most important activity of the minister as pastoral director is "edification" of a community, and its proximate goal is "to bring into being a people of God who as a Church will serve the [ultimate] purpose of the Church in the local community and the world" (82) — that is, the increase of love for God and neighbor. Preaching, administration of the sacraments, teaching, and so forth are all done to the same proximate end: the nurture of a community that is a biblical, priestly, and teaching people. Thus, in this emerging view of ministry, Niebuhr wrote, "the Church is becoming the minister and its 'minister' is its servant, directing it in its service" (83). The internal confusion of graduate professional theological schooling could be resolved, at least in part, by letting this coherent picture of ministry as pastoral direction select and organize the specific capacities the school seeks to develop in its students.

The phrase "pastoral director" is easily misconstrued. The adjective "pastoral" is crucially important. Used alone, "director" might suggest that Niebuhr is assimilating the church to voluntary community organizations like the YMCA, and its ministers to the chief executives of such organizations. In that case, the minister's most important activity would be to devise and manage attractive programs aimed at the proximate goal of increased membership. However, Niebuhr says explicitly that the minister is a pastoral director, not a pastoral "ruler" (90), which was Gregory's metaphor. Perhaps — we may surmise — Niebuhr's pastoral director is analogous to a "spiritual director"; one doesn't have spiritual "rulers." On the other hand, the minister is described as a *pastoral* director rather than a spiritual director. That is, the minister's direction is aimed not solely at persons' life of prayer but more broadly at their common public ministry to increase love in the world, not only for God, but also for all neighbors.

Now, "if a common sense of Church is nascent among the many members of one body and if a relatively clear idea is emerging of the *one* service to be rendered by ministers in their many duties, then some common idea of a theological school ought also to be possible." Of course, such an idea could not hope to be a blueprint for every theological school, but only "a kind of general prescription of the elements every blueprint would need to provide for" (106). The "common idea" of a theological school is that it should be an "intellectual center of the Church's life."[17] Three features of Niebuhr's development of this theme are noteworthy.

First, Niebuhr's proposal clearly reflects the "Berlin" model. A theological school

> is charged with a double function. On the one hand it is that place or occasion where the Church exercises its intellectual love of God and neighbor; on the other hand it is the community that serves the Church's other activities by bringing reflection and criticism to bear on worship, preaching, teaching and the care of souls. (110)

Thus, on the one hand, it shares the church's ultimate purpose, increase of love for God and neighbor, but in the intellectual mode. In exercising "intellectual love of God and neighbor," the theological school "compares, abstracts, relates; by these means it seeks coherence in the manifoldness of human experience, unified understanding of the objects or the Other in that experience. It also undertakes to correct through criticism." It engages in *Wissenschaft*. It is "pure science, disinterested as all pure science is disinterested" (108-9). It is graduate education.

On the other hand, it is also professional education. It prepares leadership for the churches by equipping persons with capacities to pursue the proximate and ultimate goals of ministry in a reflective and self-critical manner. This twofold function inevitably creates tensions, a situation not unique to theological schools. Niebuhr notes that in having this double function theological schools simply reflect the double way in which all schools are related to the societies in which they work (cf. 48). However,

---

17. Niebuhr, *The Purpose of the Church and Its Ministry*, p. 107; emphasis omitted. Note that Niebuhr did not say that a theological school should be *the* center of the church. That function does not define a theological school, according to Niebuhr.

he is emphatic in his judgment that theological schools are less bothered by this tension than they ought to be because they have chosen "to devote themselves primarily to the second," the professional school function. "They tend in consequence to neglect the first function of a theological school — the exercise of the intellectual love of God and neighbor" (49). While firmly endorsing the "Berlin" model of excellence in theological education, Niebuhr is clearly wishing polemically to weight the *Wissenschaft* side of that model and to counter a perceived tendency to put too much weight on the "professional" side.

Second, Niebuhr proposes to ground the integral unity of a school's course of study in the social dynamics of the school as a community, a "*collegium* or colleagueship" (117). It is striking that he does not ground that unity immediately in the ministerial duties for which the school prepares leadership insofar as these duties fall into a coherent pattern around a pastoral director's proximate goal of nurturing community. It is just as striking that he does not ground that unity in the structure of a theological school's object.

Like any *Wissenschaft*, a theological school's inquiries do have a determinate object: God. However, God is not known in isolation. Hence "the complex object of theological study always has the three aspects of God in relation to man, of men in relation to God, and of men-before-God in relation to each other." Accordingly "the method of such study consists of intensive participation in the life of the Biblical, historical and contemporary churches in their encounters with God and interactions with the 'world'" (125). Note the word *churches*. Given that, when God is the object of inquiry, the object is complex in this threefold way, the subject matter of inquiry is a set of "churches in their encounters with God and interactions with the 'world.'" This requires the mastery and use of the disciplines of the biblical scholar and the historian and the study of psychological, social, and cultural realities. But the focus of scholarly attention is on the churches, communities whose ultimate purpose is to increase love of God and neighbor.

Nonetheless, for Niebuhr not even this singleness of object and focus is the ground of the unity of a theological school's course of study. Rather, "the course of study is a course of constant conversation with members of a wide circle of men who live in community with God and with neighbors-before-God" (119). Indeed, it is precisely this communication that makes it a school: "Every genuine school is such a society in which the movement of communication runs back and forth among the three — the teacher, the student and the common object" (117). Note what Niebuhr appears to do here. He seems to ground the unity of a theological course of study in the coherence or integral unity of the dynamics that make a school — any type of school — a genuine school. These dynamics are discovered social-psychologically rather than theologically. It is not anything about *theos* but something about the dynamics of a distinctive type of society that is the basis of unity in a theological course of study.

This, in turn, has implications for the type of excellence in teachers that theological schools should seek. When we recall that the "common object" is itself threefold, this unifying "movement of communication" turns out to be an even more complex dynamic. It is not simply a movement among student, common object, and teachers taken one by one. Rather, it is a movement among students (themselves persons-before-God), the threefold common object (God-in-relation-to-persons; persons-in-relation-to-God; persons-before-God-in-relation-to-each-other), and teachers who are each particularly proficient in the disciplines needed for critical inquiry into one or another of the threefold aspects of the common object. Indeed, as we saw, the analysis in *The Advancement of Theological Education* concluded that it is particularly urgent that there be cross-disciplinary conversation *among* teachers. It is the entire dynamic of that conversation that makes the school's course of study an integral whole.

The third noteworthy feature of a theological school as an "intellectual center of the Church's life" is that its intellectual work is at once disinterestedly theoretical and driven by a passionate interest. According to the "Berlin" model, excellent theological schooling requires two foci: education for professional ministerial leadership and critical theological inquiry. Niebuhr insists that both poles are thoroughgoingly theoretical: "Whether its function as the exercise of the intellectual love of God and man or as the illumination of other church activities is stressed, in either case the work of the school is theoretical" (125). Like all pure science, this theoretical work is disinterested in the sense of "seeking to put aside all extraneous, private and personal interests while it concentrates on its objects for their own sake only" (109).

At the same time, like all inquiry, it is guided by an interest. A theological school's theoretical work is guided by the interest called "love of God and neighbor-before-God." This distinguishes the theoretical work of a theological school from all other forms of critical inquiry, even those that use the same disciplines in regard to what appear to be the same objects of inquiry. It distinguishes theological inquiry from "all intellectual activity guided by love of self or love of neighbor-without-God" (109). Furthermore, it distinguishes theological inquiry from intellectual activities that may be motivated by love of God and neighbor but that abstract their objects from their God-relatedness, "focusing attention on some part or aspect of creation without making them objects of devotion" (109-10).

These two aspects of a theological school's theoretical work — its necessary *dis*interestedness and its necessary guidance by interest in God — do not conflict with each other but rather require each other. For Niebuhr, that fact establishes the relationship between theological schools and the church. Church and theological school have the same ultimate purpose: the increase of love for God intellectually — that is, to know God. This purpose requires disinterested, self-critical theoretical inquiry. Hence, education to prepare leadership for the church's task of increasing love for God and neighbor must consist in disinterested theoretical activity. Such a school, clearly, is "not Church in its wholeness. It is not even the intellect of the Church" (108). It is simply an intellectual center, not even *the* intellectual center, of the church. Intellectual love is, after all, only one aspect of love for God.

On the other hand, for Niebuhr, disinterested theoretical inquiry to understand God and neighbors in their God-relatedness requires guidance by love for God in order to remain disinterested. Such inquiry needs an intellectual love for God to identify, correct for, and displace love of self and neighbor-as-related-to-self. Furthermore, intellectual love for God requires the larger context of a whole person's wholehearted love for God to sustain it precisely as intellectual love. Love for God with the mind, separated from love for God with the rest of the self, quickly ceases to be genuinely intellectual love. Hence, schooling to prepare leadership for the church must "be carried on in the context of the Church's whole life; hence those whose special duty it is to do this work must participate in that life if they are to discharge their peculiar duty" (128).

Critique

Thus Niebuhr moves to correct the problem in the revisions of the "Berlin" model of excellent theological schooling that we noted in the earlier reflections of Harper, Kelly, and Brown on North American Protestant theological education. He undertakes the task they abandoned of providing a specifically theological account of the subject matter of theological schooling's *Wissenschaft:* God in relation to neighbor; neighbor in relation to God; neighbors related to each other before God. He rejects individualistic and functionalist analyses of the ministry for which theological schools prepare leadership. He replaces those analyses with a theological analysis that is both teleological (ministry's proximate goal is to nurture church communities) and ecclesiological (the church's ultimate purpose is to increase love for God and neighbor). And he addresses the separation of *wissenschaftlich* theory and practical professional training by declaring *both* to be thoroughly theoretical and hence not separated by a difference in kind.

However, three problems haunt Niebuhr's proposal. The first has to do with the adequacy of Niebuhr's theological account of the ministry. Niebuhr's "emerging view" of the minister seems to be open to and internally unprotected from the serious threat of being taken captive ideologically as a religious sanction for a certain kind of North American middle-class life and its values. At issue is the authority by which ministry is done. Niebuhr contends that, according to the newly emerging picture of the ministry, just as "institutional authority was central in the priest's office and Scriptural in the preacher's so communal authority becomes of greatest importance to the pastoral director" (86). This does not rule out institutional authority; but it does mean that institutional authority will be exercised in a way that empowers and does not try to displace the community's capacity to govern its own life. Nor does this rule out biblical authority; but it does mean that the "minister who is obedient to Scripture and represents its authority does so as one who is interpreting the mind of the community-before-God" (87).

But is communal authority, "the mind of the community-before-God," sufficiently transcendent of the community itself to stand effectively in judgment on the community's own tendencies toward ideological complicities? Does the picture of minister as pastoral director give the minister any ground on which to stand, when such a stance is necessary, as witness to the community's ultimate purpose to increase love for God and neighbor, or to stand *over against* the community's idolatrous preoccupation with its proximate purpose to nurture community? If it is granted that there is no theological or institutional way to guarantee that church and ministry will not fall into ideological captivity, should not a theological picture of ministry more powerfully include ways in which the ultimate purpose of ministry can and must set it in tension with the concrete actuality of a particular church community at a particular time?

The bearing of this objection on this view of theological education is immediate. If the integral unity of a graduate professional theological school's course of study depends in part on the internal coherence and adequacy of a picture of the nature and purposes of ministry, then such a serious internal incoherence in the governing picture of ministry threatens the unity of the course of study.

That brings us to a second problem that haunts Niebuhr's revised version of the "Berlin" model of excellent theological schooling. When Niebuhr analyzes the causes of contradictions in theological schools' courses of study, he locates those causes in confusions in the pictures they accepted of the ministry for which they were preparing leadership. If there were a clear and coherent theological picture of the nature and purpose of ministry toward which the course of study was ordered, then, he argues, the course of study itself would become an integral whole. Fortunately, just such a picture was, he thought, then emerging: the minister as pastoral director. But when he himself addresses the issue of unity in the course of his study, he seems to ground this unity, not in this emerging picture of ministry, but in a "conversation" among students, objects of study, and faculty across disciplines. This coheres with and gives a theoretical basis for the argument Niebuhr and his fellow researchers made in *The Advancement of Theological Education* that cross-disciplinary conversation among faculty is in particular key to the recovery of unity in the course of study. In their study the authors claim to see signs of an emerging trend toward increased interdisciplinary conversation and teaching. However, whatever may have been the case about new understandings of church and ministry emerging in the mid-1950s, this trend turned out to be very short-lived. And this raises the concern that Niebuhr's approach was entirely too optimistic about what would be required to restore unity to theological schools' course of study.

It may well be that, in addition to requiring a coherent picture of ministry, recovery of unity in a course of study requires profound changes in the way in which critical inquiry is conducted in disciplined ways within theological schools. In any case, two developments since Niebuhr's study make it entirely unlikely that such changes will come about simply through academics' goodwill toward one another, interest in cross-disciplinary conversation, or openness to interdisciplinary teaching. They are sociological developments in the academic profession, in contradistinction to the ministry as a profession.

One of these developments is the burgeoning of departments of religious studies in secular colleges and universities, some with doctoral programs. Every subject matter and discipline found in the three "academic" sections of theological schools' fourfold curricula are taught in religious studies departments too. Faculty in those fields who are members of departments of religious studies receive their doctoral education in the same graduate schools as do faculty in theological schools, and faculty move back and forth between the two contexts.

The other development is the increased importance of national associations of scholars in religious studies — for example, the Society of Biblical Literature, the American Academy of Religion, and the American Society for Church History. These associations, rather than faculty members' own theological schools, are the institutions by which professional academic status and recognition are awarded and acknowledged. These organizations also provide the communications network through which schools find candidates suitable for faculty positions and through which scholars seeking new positions find schools with appropriate openings. Faculty mobility depends heavily on these organizations.

Between these two developments, theological school faculties are now far more strongly professionalized than they were when Niebuhr wrote, and the institutional framework and reference point for this professionalization lies entirely outside theological schools. This works against the idea that the faculties of theological schools have more in common with one another in a cross-disciplinary way than they have in common with colleagues in the same disciplines outside theological schools. Members of a discipline, wherever they teach, have been trained in the same graduate schools, hold themselves accountable to the same standards of academic excellence, and attend to the same agenda of issues.

It is increasingly difficult to assign any actual content to Niebuhr's distinction between intellectual work that is done in theological schools, guided by love of God and attending to its objects in their God-relatedness, and intellectual work that is either not guided by love of God or, when it is, always attends to its object in abstraction from its God-relatedness, as must be done by definition in a secular college or university. Just what difference would that distinction make to what one studies and how one researches it, to what one teaches and how one teaches it?

The increased professionalization of academic life in religious studies also works against serious faculty investment of time and energy in interdisciplinary teaching and research. The peer groups that define the issues to be explored, that award academic status, that provide access to power in the academy, and that make mobility possible are no longer comprised of one's colleagues across the disciplines within one academic institution; rather, one's peer group is comprised of one's colleagues in the same "field" or "subfield" nationally. Neither status nor power is generated by intellectual work at the edges or across the boundaries of one's field. In such a context, the sort of collegiality on which Niebuhr rests the hope of new unity in theological schools' course of study seems unlikely to develop without deep rearrangements of institutionalized power in both theological schools and the several academic specialties nationally.

Of course, Niebuhr did not expect sheer geniality to restore the unity of the course of study. His final appeal is to his doctrine of God. Disunity comes because of faculty confusion of proximate with ultimate goals; it is a result of idolatry. Unity may rest on collegiality created by conversation across disciplines, but that collegiality depends on repentance and conversion from idolatry to faith in the One beyond the many. The question is whether the requisite repentance and conversion do not need to be institutional and structural within the schools themselves in addition to being personal and individual among the members of the faculty.

The third question about Niebuhr's proposal has to do with his way of holding together the academic and the professional aspects of theological schooling. Earlier North American modifications of the "Berlin" model equated "academic" as *Wissenschaft* with "theory" and equated "professional" with "practice," and then opposed "theory" and "practice" so sharply that it was difficult to see how they could enrich or correct one another. Niebuhr, as we saw, attempts to overcome this opposition by declaring both *Wissenschaft* and professional education to be thoroughly theoretical. If there is something problematic about this, it is not the claim that both poles of graduate professional theological schooling are theoretical, but rather the concept of "theory" that is invoked.

Niebuhr recognizes that his claim requires some further explanation of the relation between theory and practice. He rejects an "intellectualist" picture according to which theory precedes action and "the movement is from . . . thought to voluntary deeds." And he rejects a "pragmatic" picture according to which theory follows action "as an affair of rationalizations, essentially irrelevant to practice" (126-27). Rather, theory and practice are intertwined, but neither is the source or end of the other: "Reflection is never the first action, though in personal and communal life we can never go back to a moment in which action has been unmodified by reflection" (127). This is true of both the academic and the professional poles of theological schooling; it is true both of study of its complex object and of reflection on and critique of churchly actions. Hence "theoretical activity can be only provisionally and partly separated from the Church's total action" (133). However, the school does not itself attempt to embrace the total action. The school is constituted by theoretical activity only and is thus dependent on the more inclusive activity of the church. Those who engage in theological schooling, students and faculty, must themselves be engaged in these more inclusive activities also, not because we learn by doing, but because "we do not learn the meaning of deeds *without* doing" (129).

This is consistent with and underwrites the insistence in *The Advancement of Theological Education* that the goal of theological schooling is to help students become self-educating. A distinctive pattern of movement in theological schooling is suggested here. We have already seen several such patterns: from source, usually Scripture, to appropriation (on the older model of paideia); from source to application in life and ministry (on a later model of paideia); from source through theory to application in ministerial practice (on the "Berlin" model); and from source through theory to popularization to ministerial application (on a revised "Berlin" model).

In Niebuhr the pattern seems to be from theory to appropriation of theory. Theological schooling is by definition a theoretical matter regarding both God and churchly activities. Students are no more "trained" in the doing of church activities than they are simply "informed" about the results of research. Rather, they are schooled in *how* to study anything critically and theoretically so that they appropriate the relevant disciplines for themselves. That way they can continue to be self-educating for the rest of their lives, including but not limited to their professional lives as ministers. Of course, they need to have experience in relevant kinds of "doing," whether in personal living or in church activities, in order to have at hand the "doing" whose meaning is to be examined critically and theoretically. But providing that experience in "doing" is not constitutive of the school; what is constitutive of the school is theoretical reflection on the meaning of the "doing" — when it is done to the end of capacitating students to continue in the same ways for the rest of their lives.

This view is worrisome because it is finally unclear about just how theory is intertwined with practice in such a way that neither is the source or end of the other. Is the intertwining a dialectical relation? Is it just an "alongsidedness"? If it is simply an alongsidedness, then theory and practice are inherently independent of one another, even though in actual fact we may never find one without the other. In that case, the distinction Niebuhr draws between the theoretical intellectual activity that constitutes a theological school and the larger activities of the church is cogent. But the confidence that theological schooling that consists entirely of theoretical work done to educate persons to be self-educating will somehow consequently shape and empower ministry seems to be simply an act of faith. No reasons are given for believing that such schooling in theoretical work is likely to have such consequences. Rather, one is simply given the observation that theoretical reflection and practical action have very often gone together. Hope for the best in the future! When part of the things one hopes for are resources for vigilant and acute identification and critique of ideological captivity both in church actions and in theological schooling, this sounds more like an invitation to genial optimism than like a grounded hope.

On the other hand, if the relation between theory and practice is genuinely a dialectical one, we have strong reason for believing that education in theoretical work to equip students to be self-educating will result in focused, self-critical, and self-nurturing ministry. For then theory *by definition* presupposes some practice to be explained and criticized, and it issues in revised practice; and practice *by definition* presupposes some theory by which to assess the present situation calling for action, and it issues in theorizing about what happened and what to do next. If this is the case, however, then Niebuhr's restriction of theological schooling to theoretical work seems artificial and inappropriately abstract. If theory and practice are intertwined in a dialectical way, then to engage in one is inescapably to engage in the other also, as an inherent part of education. So this dialectical view is also problematic, and it fails to allay our worries about Niebuhr's vague relation of theory to practice.

Wissenschaft and Excellence in Theological Schooling

Taken together, these studies of theological schooling at once exhibit and partly explain the firm grip of the "Berlin" model of excellence in education on American Protestant theological schools and the problems it creates for them. Unlike the Kelly and May-Brown studies, there is little evidence that the Niebuhr-Williams-Gustafson study had long-lasting influence on North American theological schooling. It is as though the study brought to explicit articulation the theological underpinnings of the practice of theological schooling then at its peak. It is probable that the views articulated in the study are still the theological views that mainline Protestant theological educators are most likely to offer as a theological account of their enterprise. Perhaps a retrospective look from a greater historical perspective will show that the Niebuhr report reflects the end of a phenomenon of which William Rainey Harper's study marked the beginning: the influence on Protestant theological schooling of major themes in the "progressivist era" in American cultural history. We do not yet have enough historical distance to judge such matters. What we do have through the Niebuhr-Williams-Gustafson study, as through its predecessors, is clear evidence of the power of the "Berlin" *Wissenschaft-cum*-professional school model of excellence in schooling over North American theological schools.

In particular, these studies of the "Berlin" model of excellence suggest several morals and cautions about any effort to analyze and understand a theological school:

- that the "Berlin" model's bipolar picture of excellent theological schooling, both *wissenschaftlich* and aimed at preparing leadership for "professional ministry," is a deeply institutionalized reality in American Protestant theological schools and cannot be changed or left behind easily;
- that the institutionalization of the "Berlin" model in theological schooling rewards an individualistic picture of teaching and research and works against collegial and cross-disciplinary teaching and research;
- that *Wissenschaft* — that is, critical, disciplined, theoretical thinking — is a powerful weapon against (though no

guarantee of escape from) ideological distortions in efforts to understand;

- that in the context of *theological* schooling *Wissenschaft* is a powerful tool against the religious idolatry of ideological captivity and distortion, both in efforts to understand theology's object and in the practice of ministry;

- that *Wissenschaft* and education for "professional" ministry tend to be increasingly alienated from each other the more professional ministry is understood in an individualistic and functionalist manner, and that only *Wissenschaft* is understood to be "theoretical";

- and finally, that it is particularly important to be critically attentive to the concepts of "theory" and "practice" that are employed by any proposal seeking to understand a theological school, and that it is also important to pay attention to the proposal's assumptions about human personhood.

This model does not cohere easily with the paideia model of excellent theological schooling. Until recently there has been no discussion of theological schooling in which the strengths and problems of the two models were explicitly engaged with each other. And yet theological schools in North America are inescapably driven to try to meet standards set both by paideia and by the research university as models of excellence in schooling. As we have seen, the standards associated with paideia impose themselves simply because the picture of Christianity as itself a kind of paideia is historically so deeply rooted. The standards associated with the research university are imposed, if in no other way, by the decision to meet the accepted standards for accreditation of graduate professional schools. These include the criteria that the academic program be at a "postgraduate" level — that is, that students have completed an undergraduate degree; that there be a certain level of library holdings; that faculty members themselves hold graduate "research" degrees; that there be provisions protecting academic freedom such as academic tenure; and so forth. The reward system for faculty further underscores research university values, since promotion and the possibility of moving to a faculty appointment in another institution tend to rest on criteria rooted in the "guild" of fellow researchers in the same field of inquiry rather than in the common life of any given school. Both the accrediting of the school and the self-identity of the scholar are sustained by traffic coming down the Berlin Turnpike.

The two models sit together very uneasily. The tension between them is never resolved, and no theological school escapes struggles created by the tension between them. There can only be various sorts of negotiated truces between the two incommensurate sets of criteria of excellence in schooling.

There is something like a spectrum of these truces. At either end are theological schools that come close to being pure instances of one model or the other. Thus there are schools in which paideia's focus on students' understanding of God plays almost no role whatever, neither in shaping what is taught and how, nor in the conventions governing how faculty and students interrelate, how faculty are selected, and how the school manages its common life. In contrast, there are also schools in which, aside from meeting minimal standards for accreditation, no role is given to the research university's emphasis on original contributions to knowledge, freedom of learning, and freedom to research.

More common are schools in which some compromise has been worked out between the two models. It may be an arrangement that factors out different aspects of the school's common life to the reign of each model of excellent schooling: the research university model may reign for faculty, for example, or for faculty in certain fields (say, church history, or biblical studies) but not in others (say, practical theology), while paideia reigns as the model for students, or only for students with a declared vocation to ordained ministry (so that other students aspiring to graduate school are free to attempt to meet standards set by the research university model); or research university values may be celebrated in relation to the school's official "academic" program, including both classroom expectations and the selection and rewarding of faculty, while the school's extracurricular life is shaped by commitments coming from the model provided by paideia so that, for example, common worship is made central to their common life and a high premium is placed on the school being a residential community. Clearly, the possible ways to parcel out the common life of a theological school between the two models are endless in number.

The current discussion of what's theological about theological education can be read as the first discussion of theological schooling in which both models of excellence are explicitly engaged. Seen in one way, each of the participants in the discussion attempts to work out some sort of compromise between the two models. Seen in another way, some participants can be read as adopting one of the models and attempting to incorporate the best features of the other, but on terms dictated by the privileged model; some try to do the reverse. That raises the question whether there might be some third possible picture of excellence altogether. It is to that current discussion that we turn in the next chapter.

4

"Athens": Unity and Pluralism in the Current Discussion

A conversation has been going on in North America concerning what is theological about theological education. It is not only the longest-lived but by far the liveliest conversation theological educators have ever managed to sustain among themselves ecumenically about the nature and purpose of their common enterprise. It has produced an unprecedented amount of publication about the topic. In this literature the models of excellence for theological schooling provided by "Athens" and "Berlin" engage each other for the first time, sometimes working out compromises, and always showing in bold relief an array of basic issues confronting every theological school.

There are two broad types of issues. It has been convenient, though misleading, to tag them as issues about unity and issues about pluralism in theological schools.[1] They both have to do

1. Cf. David H. Kelsey and Barbara G. Wheeler, "Mind-Reading: Notes on the Basic Issues Program," *Theological Education* 20, 2 (Spring 1984): 8-14;

with the nature of the "Christian thing" and how theological education is related to the "Christian thing." "Unity" issues tie into this question: "Is this theological school's course of study adequate to the inherent unity (or 'integrity' or 'identity') of the 'Christian thing'?" "Pluralism" issues tie into this question: "Is this theological school's course of study adequate to the pluralistic world in which 'the Christian thing' is actually lived?" When the answer to either of these questions is "No!" then this issue arises: Is it something about our understanding of "theological school" or of the "Christian thing" or of how they are related that creates these inadequacies?

Note that basic issues about theological schools tend to be conceptual and theoretical in character. They have to do with the ways in which we explicitly or implicitly understand various matters. There are also, of course, practical problems raised by the same questions, such as these: *How* do we make a course of study more adequate to the pluralism of the world in which the "Christian thing" is lived without so overloading the curriculum as to make it inadequate to the inherent unity of the "Christian thing"? *How* do we find faculty who not only are masters of their academic specializations but also see how those specializations bear on the "Christian thing" in its integrity and fit together with other specializations in doing so? *How* pluralistic should the student body of this theological school be, or, for that matter, its faculty, etc.? Individual theological schools must debate and solve such problems all the time. They must do so in reference to the factors that make them the concretely particular schools they are — their peculiar histories, governance structures, social and economic location, and the like.

The point is that in all such debates some conceptual and

David H. Kelsey, "Reflections on Convocation '84: Issues in Theological Education," *Theological Education* 21, 2 (Spring 1985): 116-31.

theoretical framework is at least tacitly employed. The *basic* issues tending these debates have to do with the adequacy of that assumed framework and whether it may in fact subtly confuse the debate or help to cause the problem in the first place. Whereas the "problems" faced by theological schools are practical matters needing solutions, the "issues" confronting them are conceptual matters needing resolutions. It is with issues rather than problems that the current discussion has concerned itself. This understandably makes persons who feel the urgent need to solve problems impatient with the conversation. However, the conversation about basic issues promises to yield something like a therapy that, if stayed with over time, will help to clarify which problems are most important, why some problems may turn out to be less important than they first seemed, why others chronically prove to be intractable, and just what is at stake in the "real" problems.

Clearly the words *unity* and *pluralism* may easily mislead because they are both vague and ambiguous. That does not require us to abandon them but only to use them with care to designate the two broad ranges of basic issues in the current discussion of what's theological about theological schools. It is necessary only to sort out as clearly as possible the various senses in which each could be used and then to be clear about which sense we intend. It will be useful to us later on if we do a bit of preliminary sorting out now before moving on to the discussion proper.

To begin with, consider this question: "Is this theological school's course of study adequate to the inherent unity of the 'Christian thing'?" The meaning of *unity* depends on our construal of the "Christian thing." Is the "Christian thing" like a coherent body of doctrines, with the sort of unity appropriate to a body of theory? Or is it more like a way of being a human person, with the sort of unity appropriate to personal identity? Or is it more like a set of moral rules, with the unity appropriate

97

to a code of law? Or is it more like a system of cultural symbols, with the sort of unity appropriate to a single culture?

Then consider this similar question: "Is this theological school's course of study adequate to the pluralistic world in which the 'Christian thing' is lived?" A "pluralism" of what? The meaning of *pluralism* depends in part on the way in which one understands "world." Perhaps we intend a pluralism of cultures. In that case, we construe "world" as the planet earth and analyze its population into various "cultures," each of which is relatively homogeneous and has a recognizable identity. Then, in jargon currently fashionable among theological educators, we speak of basic issues raised in the effort to "globalize" theological schooling and the effort to "contextualize" the "Christian thing" in culture after culture.

Perhaps we intend a pluralism of religions. In that case we construe "world" as a realm of religious symbols, practices, experiences, and institutions, including Christian ones. Then we speak of issues raised in efforts at interreligious dialogue. These may or may not be the same as issues raised in efforts to contextualize and globalize theological education; there are, after all, more dimensions to "other" cultures than their religious dimensions.

Perhaps, however, we intend a pluralism of social "locations." In that case we construe "world" as "social reality" and analyze the way in which persons' experience and knowledge are shaped by the sexual, racial, and economic factors that determine their locations in their society's structure of status and power. Then we speak of issues raised in efforts to bring the "Christian thing" to bear on their distinctive modes of experience and knowledge.

As they bear on a theological school, these and other sorts of pluralism interrelate in complex and confusing ways. One central confusion has to do with the possibility of conflict. It is debatable whether certain sorts of pluralism create an adversarial situation for the "Christian thing." For example, it is an ongoing debate whether religious pluralism creates competition and even conflict for the "Christian thing." So too, it can be debated whether the "Christian thing" is necessarily in deep conflict with any given culture in which it is being contextualized. However, it cannot be debated that certain sorts of social location *demand* to be resisted and changed — namely, unjust locations that oppress the people who live in them. Attending to this sort of pluralism raises a different order of basic issues for a theological school than does attention to other sorts of pluralism.

Put abstractly, each of these "worlds" is pluralized by different *interests*. That is what makes it superficially appropriate to refer to a pluralism as a plurality of "interest groups." However, "interest group" suggests interests of a self-aggrandizing sort, and that is entirely unjust. To be sure, the interests that define many groups are interests to maintain and preserve traditions of belief and action, symbols and aspirations that are held dear. Often they are patterns of belief and action from which the groups benefit. Such is the case with cultural and religious pluralism. However, some groups are defined by interests to change social structures and to be liberated from their bondage. Neither interest in maintaining what is held dear nor interest in liberation from what is oppressive need be an interest in self-aggrandizement; both may be rooted in a universalizable picture of the good life, an interest in human flourishing. When we deal with pluralism defined by the latter sort of interest, however, we must speak of issues raised for a theological school by the effort to address this pluralism in an actually liberating way, not simply in a theoretical way.

The ambiguity of the concept of "pluralism" is further complexified by the fact that a theological school itself is a pluralistic world in all of these senses. When that pluralism is in view, we must speak of issues raised for theological education by the effort to make the course of study adequate to the school's *own* internal pluralisms.

"Unity" and "pluralism" are not polar opposites, and to raise issues about one is not antithetical to raising issues about the other. That is, the quest for unity in a theological course of study is not an effort to overcome pluralism and its consequences. Pluralism is not necessarily another name for self-contradiction and fragmentation in theological schooling, a problem to which unity is the solution. Nor is the quest for an adequate response to pluralism an effort to overcome unity. Unity is not necessarily another name for narrowness and bias in theological schooling, a problem to which pluralism is the answer. If one attends to issues raised by the quest for unity, one does not imply that it is misguided to raise issues about pluralism; nor does a focus on issues raised by the quest to be adequate to pluralism imply that it is a sign of evasion or confusion to raise issues about unity.

*   *   *

In the remainder of this chapter and in the following chapters I want to show what difference the differences among three distinguishable approaches make in the current conversation. The first approach accords with the "Athens" type and explicitly or implicitly adopts paideia as the model of excellence in theological schooling, while incorporating the best of the "Berlin" type. However, one representative (Edward Farley in *Theologia* and *The Fragility of Knowledge*)[2] uses this approach to address issues concerning unity in theological schooling, while another (the Mud Flower Collective in *God's Fierce Whimsy*)[3] relies on it to address issues concerning pluralism.

The second approach, explored in the next chapter, accords with the "Berlin" type and explicitly or implicitly adopts *Wissen-*

2. Farley, *Theologia: The Fragmentation and Unity of Theological Education* (Philadelphia: Fortress Press, 1983), and *The Fragility of Knowledge: Theological Education in the Church and the University* (Philadelphia: Fortress Press, 1988).

3. *God's Fierce Whimsy* (New York: Pilgrim Press, 1985).

schaft and "professional" schooling as the model of excellence in theological education, while incorporating the best of the "Athens" type. However, one representative study (Joseph C. Hough, Jr., and John B. Cobb, Jr.'s *Christian Identity and Theological Education*)[4] uses this approach to address issues concerning unity, while another (Max L. Stackhouse's *Apologia*)[5] relies on it to address issues concerning pluralism.

A third approach (represented by Charles Wood in *Vision and Discernment*)[6] can be read as an attempt to formulate a third model of excellent schooling in a way that addresses issues of unity and pluralism in their basic interconnectedness. We shall discuss this approach in Chapter 6. The structure of these three chapters simply mirrors the three steps in a dialectic among these three approaches.

Unity with Pluralism in Accord with "Athens": Edward Farley

It is fair to say that Edward Farley's *Theologia,* the first extended North American theological reflection on theological education since H. Richard Niebuhr's study almost thirty years before, launched the current discussion. The basic issue to which he addressed himself in that book, and in the collection of essays that make up its sequel, *The Fragility of Knowledge,* is the fragmentation of theological education. This fragmentation has resulted from distortions that have corrupted both poles of the dominant "Berlin" model of excellent theological schooling. The "professional schooling" pole has equated "professional" with

---

4. Hough and Cobb, *Christian Identity and Theological Education* (Chico: Scholars Press, 1985).

5. Stackhouse, *Apologia: Contextualization, Globalization, and Mission in Theological Education* (Grand Rapids: William B. Eerdmans, 1988).

6. Wood, *Vision and Discernment* (Atlanta: Scholars Press, 1985).

"clergy functions." It has redefined "theology" as the theory to be "applied" in successful performance of those functions. For its part, the *wissenschaftlich* pole is inherently "tragic,"[7] inherently open to deformity. This is because, in order to make headway toward knowledge, it must distort its object of knowledge by abstracting it from its concrete setting. That distortion can be corrected by conjoining specialized research with "perspectives" on all knowledge that offer synoptic interpretations in which the objects of research are returned to their larger physical and social settings. Farley particularly notes the perspectives provided by "intuitive imagination," "tradition," and "praxis" (*Fragility*, 6). However, those perspectives have been so marginalized in the modern research university that they are unable to play their corrective role, and thus *Wissenschaft* is left fragmented.[8]

Together, these distortions of the "Berlin" model leave theological schooling bereft of its proper center: *theologia*. Farley uses the term *theologia* rather than *theology* in order to underline that it is a kind of wisdom and not, as *theology* tends to suggest, a body of information and theory about God. In *Theologia* Farley argues that this center can be recovered and the fragmentation of theological education can be overcome only by a recovery of a modified version of paideia as the mode of theological schooling. In *The Fragility of Knowledge* he goes on to argue that there is a structure to this theological study that is dictated by the essential nature of *theologia* — that is, a structure that has a theological rationale. His suggestions about how fragmentation might be overcome and how a suitable structure could be restored to theological schooling "are intended to be of sufficient ecumenical character to be pertinent to theological schools of

7. Farley, *Fragility*, p. 31; subsequent citations will be given parenthetically in the text.

8. Farley develops this theme in the first three chapters of *Fragility*.

different denominations and even different branches of Christendom."[9]

Definitions

Clearly, it is of the utmost importance to understand what *theologia* is. *Theologia* is rooted in and rises out of faith's situation. Thus *theologia* must be understood in terms of its relation to faith. What is faith? "Faith describes the way in which the human being lives in and toward God and the world under the impact of redemption."[10] This is Farley's characterization of the "Christian thing." Faith itself is a kind of knowing. "Redemption" impacts persons' lives through what Farley calls "the total mythos of the Christian faith" or the "faith-world": images, doctrines, and forms of communal life, and the "realities" carried by these images, doctrines, and the like (*Theologia,* 166). As life under the impact of redemption, faith is inherently *prereflectively* "insightful" or "cognitive" (cf. 156-57). On the other hand, persons of faith also exist "in an already disposed biographical, social and historical situation" (165). They are concretely located. Thus, on this view the "Christian thing" has the sort of unity that belongs to a distinctive way of being "set" into the world and the distinctive perspective on the world that that affords.

Assuming that this is an acceptable description of faith, how is *theologia* related to it? Farley contends that *theologia* must be characterized in two ways. Looked at in one way, *theologia* is something like a believer's settled disposition to do certain things or to act in specific ways. The classical name for such a disposition is *habitus.* Looked at in another way, *theologia* is a "dialectical activity" in which a believer engages. These are not two different sorts of theology. Rather, theology properly understood is so

9. Farley, *Theologia,* p. 151; subsequent citations will be given parenthetically in the text.
10. Farley, *Theologia,* p. 156; cf. *Fragility,* pp. 137-38, for amplification.

complex a reality as to require these two descriptions if it is to be characterized adequately. Each description, however, relates *theologia* to faith in a different way.

Considered as a *habitus, theologia* seems to be distinct from faith, just as the end state of a process is distinct from its beginning state. More exactly, *theologia* seems to be a set of different modes of this *habitus*. To call *theologia* a *habitus* is to liken it to those moral virtues that were formed through classical paideia. A moral virtue was classically understood to be a settled disposition or *habitus* to act in specific morally valued ways — for example, prudently or courageously. By analogy, *theologia* is a "cognitive [rather than moral] disposition and orientation of the soul" (*Theologia*, 35). In Farley's view, faith is inherently driven to subject itself to "deliberate processes of reflection and inquiry" through which its prereflective insightfulness becomes reflective and self-conscious insightfulness. The reflective wisdom at which faith arrives at the end of this process is *theologia. Theologia* is not related to faith in an "about" mode, as a description is related to the thing described. No, *theologia* is a personal wisdom, a way of being human, not information or theory *about* a way of being human.

And it comes in several modes. This complicates the notion of *habitus*. Just as faith always has some particular situation, so the *habitus* that is rooted in it has some particular social setting or matrix. Farley notes three such matrices, none of which is mutually exclusive. One is the situation of the believer as such. This varies enormously across cultures and epochs, but it does have some "perennial elements" (*Theologia*, 157). Farley especially stresses forces in the situation that corrupt and oppress human life and faith itself. Such forces require faith to become critically self-vigilant and hence self-reflective about both itself and its situation.

A second matrix for this *habitus* is the situation of leadership in the church, either ordained or not. Although this matrix, too, varies enormously, all instances of it have in common the aim to gather the community of faith to function as a redemptive community. This will yield a different mode of *theologia* than that of the believer as such (including the leader's own), but without displacing it, because it "aims to evoke the believer's understanding and action" (*Theologia*, 158).

A third matrix of this *habitus* is inquiry and scholarship. Its social context "is usually, but not necessarily, the school. The task is the determination or uncovering of truth" in orderly, disciplined, and systematic ways. Here *theologia* exists in a third mode as "theological knowledge." In every mode, as faith's prereflective insightfulness is brought to reflective insightfulness, *theologia* is wisdom and understanding; but only in the matrix of *Wissenschaft* is it knowledge. This mode of *theologia* does not replace or exclude either of the other two. Presumably it could be expected to help empower those in leadership settings for the mode of understanding they require there; hence the value that is placed on *Wissenschaft* in theological schooling (*Theologia*, 159).

Considered as a "dialectical activity," on the other hand, *theologia* seems to be not the end point of a process but the process itself. Here *theologia* simply *is* "that dialectic of understanding which is evoked by faith's attempt to exist faithfully in its situations" (*Theologia*, 169). Looked at in this way, *theologia* seems to be faith's own internal *process* of becoming reflective. This process has several moments.

First is the "thematization of the faith-world" (*Theologia*, 166). By "faith-world" Farley means that complex of images, doctrines, and forms of communal life, and the "realities" they carry, "in" which, in a manner of speaking, persons of faith live unreflectively and naively most of the time. The entire complex shapes the way they construe themselves and the world, other persons and God in relation to themselves. For the most part this complex is too close to consciousness to be explicitly describable. To "thematize" the complex is to gain some distance on it and at least outline its principal motifs and patterns. Thematization needs to be done so that persons of faith can use the symbols and practices of the "Christian mythos" to read the situation in which they find themselves. However, there will be a tendency to grant the situation the status of a norm by which to assess the mythos (e.g., "These biblical notions are irrelevant, meaningless, or false *because* they don't cohere with our modern worldview").

Hence, a second moment "intervenes." The situation "viewed in relation to the transcendent" (*Theologia,* 166) is seen both as creaturely, requiring a repudiation of its claim to absoluteness, and as corrupted, requiring theological criticism. However, by the same token, faith refuses *all* absolutizations, not only of various situations, but also of the total mythos itself.

So a third moment involves a "distancing and criticism in relation to tradition itself" to unmask "the elements in the tradition which serve oppression, ideology and the legitimation of privilege" (*Theologia,* 167). Left at that, however, *theologia* as a dialectical activity would be in the bind of interpreting the "total mythos of Christian faith" as at once normative for critique of the tradition and yet itself open to critique because it is relative to particular historical and cultural conditions.

Accordingly, a fourth moment "surmounts this impasse and grasps the mythos in its enduring reality and its power" (*Theologia,* 167). It discerns what it is about the mythos that "expresses enduring truth . . . about God and the presence of God" and hence about "what the world is and what human being is." In short, it discerns "the kingdom of God" — that is, "*the situation* [which is what the dialectic first set out to read] as God undergirds it, pervades it, disposes it, lures it to its best possibilities" (168).

Together, the views of *theologia* as a *habitus* and as a dialectical activity entail, not "the idea of a university," but at least the rudiments of "the idea of a theological school." That is, they entail the rudiments of the essence of any school that is entitled to consider itself a "matrix" for education of church leadership. To be sure, in both books Farley is centrally concerned to insist that the "theological education" whose unity he seeks to restore is something that *also* takes place outside theological schools and must not be identified with theological schooling. It may equally well take place in the churches and in college and university departments of religious studies. Nonetheless, his argument does in fact imply the rudiments of the essence of a theological school, which is our focus. This can be brought out by considering the three elements Farley distinguishes in theological schooling: *theologia*, pedagogy, and scholarship.

The Structure of Theological Education: Theologia, Habitus, *and Paideia*

If *theologia* is a cognitive *habitus* analogous to moral virtue, then necessarily "the education that serves it," like the education that forms moral virtue, "has the character of paideia" (*Theologia,* 178). This is its proper pedagogy. Hence, theological schooling is a form of paideia. Like moral virtue, *theologia* cannot be taught directly; this paideia requires the teacher to be midwife of a wisdom that only faith can give. While a number of things may be studied directly, such study can only be the occasion for the evocation of *theologia.*

Like classical paideia, which shapes persons' lives morally, this paideia is done for its own sake. This fact addresses one of the causes of fragmentation by excluding from the outset any definition of theological schooling by reference to the cultivation of skills whose ultimate payoff lies in "successful" clerical practice. One of Farley's major points is that this paideia is not to be simply identified with *clergy* education. Theological education is one selfsame thing. It may take place in a variety of settings, only one of which may be clergy education. It is one selfsame paideia whether it occurs in the context of a congregation, a theological seminary, or a college or university department of religious studies. The logic of the claim seems to go something like this: *Theologia* is one selfsame *habitus* in all persons who have it because it is rooted in one selfsame faith that marks them all as, precisely, believers — albeit believers located in diverse situations. Consequently, the paideia through which that *habitus* is nurtured in people is itself one selfsame process of "theological education." Hence, theological schooling is basically the *same pedagogy* (paideia) in all times and places.

At the same time, as we saw, Farley stresses that different social settings (that of the believer, the church leader, the scholar) yield different modes of the *habitus*. This creates space, as Christian appropriation of classical paideia did not, for acknowledgment of legitimate pluralism in theological education. Indeed, there are two sorts of pluralism admitted here. One is a pluralism of settings for theological education. This creates a pluralism of modes of the paideia that aims at the cultivation of *theologia*. We have seen that their plurality does not necessarily create conflict among them; but it does raise the question of how this plurality coheres with the postulated self-identity of the paideia across all its various settings. The other type of pluralism occurs within one of the matrices of *theologia* — namely, the situations of believers as such. These vary enormously. The major determinants of this pluralism are believers' race, gender, and "location" socially, economically, culturally, and historically. This variety might very well entail unavoidable conflict among deeply different versions of "faith." It raises a question about the unity of the "Christian thing" and how it coheres with this pluralism of believers' situations.

In sum, by construing *theologia* as *habitus*, Farley moves to correct one cause of the malaise of theological schooling: the amalgamation of questions of pedagogy with questions of scholarship while *theologia* is totally ignored. In Farley's proposal, the very nature of *theologia* dictates that its proper pedagogy be defined neither by the demands of clergy functions nor by the demands of scholarship; as a *habitus, theologia* itself demands paideia as its pedagogy. At the same time, the inescapably situated character of the *habitus* entails a revision of the classical idea of paideia to acknowledge that it exists concretely in a plurality of modes.

If *theologia* is a dialectical activity, then necessarily the education that serves it must be disciplined and critical, and classical paideia must be radically modified in another way. As we saw, the dialectic inherently requires a pedagogy that in disciplined fashion critically tests for truth and for ideology, both in faith's situation and in the Christian mythos. Further, Farley contends, the structure of the dialectic entails a structure or order to the pedagogy. Accordingly, a theological school will *necessarily* involve critical inquiry that exhibits a certain order or structure.

What counts as "critical" reflection has, Farley holds, been irrevocably changed since the Enlightenment through a "massive, centuries-long paradigm shift from ahistorical to historical ways of understanding reality" (*Fragility*, 119). Classical paideia studies its subject matter ahistorically. Even Newman's nineteenth-century version of paideia, though it had room for critical history, still founded the structure of the course of study in an ahistorical essential structure of reality. If paideia now must understand everything historically, it can no longer be a movement from a source that is beyond critique to application. The "source" itself, Scripture and the total Christian mythos, must be critically studied historically. That immediately undercuts the classical employment of a fourfold structure of the course of study that moved from Scripture (source) studies through history and dogmatics to practical theology.

However, *theologia* as a dialectical activity provides a substitute structure for a theological school's course of study. "Structure, here, means the areas of study that theology . . . requires, and the relation between those areas" (*Fragility*, 171; cf. 104-5). This requires further analysis of what faith is. The structure of theological study must be dictated, not by pedagogical considerations, nor by the conditions necessary for scholarship, but by the essential nature of faith — or, more exactly, faith-within-its-situations modified by a particular matrix. This has to be explained in greater detail.

As we have seen, for Farley "faith . . . is a way of having, living in, and responding to situations," characterized in its particularly Christian form as "existence . . . in the mode of redemption" (*Fragility,* 137). It is always located in some concrete situation:

> working in a factory, shopping, worshiping, attending a concert, living in a family. These situations are less amalgams of contents presented to our cognition than they are composite *dimensions* to be understood and interpreted. Dimensions here are aspects of a situation which differ from one another in genre or type. (135-36)

Faith is not itself "a discrete life situation but a way of being in life situations." Nor does it replace the dimensions of any life situation. Rather, "faith brings new features to every situation . . . — new dimensions opened up by redemption itself and how it occurs" (137). These include a community ("ecclesia") and its tradition (the total Christian mythos); the "imagery and vision of the goodness, fragility, corruption, and hope of the human condition under the transcendent (the gospel); and . . . a praxis-oriented existence" (action).[11]

Farley is careful to stress that these dimensions introduced into every situation by faith "are not simply something 'subjective,' at the consciousness pole, although the emphasis is certainly on the believer." All of them presuppose a "condition, reality, or reference of redemptive existence" that is objective (*Fragility,* 143-44). We might name that objective pole "God" or "Word of God." How-

11. Farley, *Fragility,* pp. 137-38.

ever, this objective pole is never immediately available for study. We can hope to come to understand "It" only by way of study of what mediates "It" — namely, the Christian faith. Hence, the Christian faith within its various situations is "the most general subject matter, the content, of theological study" (144). But that does not yet dictate the structure of the course of study.

It is "the aims rather than the subject matter of theological study [that] provide the initial *clues*" (*Fragility*, 103; emphasis added) to the structure of its course of study, and it is those aims that provide its unity (173). These aims are dictated by what faith itself requires to be done to this subject matter: *interpretation*. Here is where we get to the structure of theological study. As we have seen, faith inherently drives itself from prereflective insightfulness to reflective insightfulness through a four-moment dialectical activity called *theologia*. Each moment of that dialectic turns on acts of interpretation. Different types of interpretation are called for by the different types or dimensions of faith's situations, including the dimensions that faith itself introduces. Accordingly,

> the *aim* of theological study is to discipline, or rigorize, the basic modes of interpretation that already exist in the situation of faith, and . . . these hermeneutic [i.e., interpretative] modes generate the requisites and criteria for the areas of study and the movement of study in the field.[12]

---

12. Farley, *Fragility*, p. 171. Here it is worth noting some technical distinctions Farley draws among "pedagogical areas," "sciences," "specialty fields," and "perspectival emphases" (cf. *Fragility*, pp. 33-35, 109). *Pedagogical areas* are defined by the aims of teaching. Each one is a subject matter located within a larger arrangement of other subject matters, the whole of which is structured in a way that reflects the aims of teaching. Examples would be "cooking, auto mechanics, and reading."

Sciences are defined by their objects and their methods of research. The "objects" are selected because they are problematic, the methods because they are appropriate to the sorts of problems the objects present. Sciences are not defined by the aims of teaching. They require some sort of institutional location whose

Farley proposes that the aim to discipline the basic modes of interpretation already present in faith's "dialectical activity" — that is, *theologia* — provides a way both to restructure and to reunify the theological course of study on *theological* grounds rather than on grounds dictated by the present disarray in the academy. Farley suggests that analysis of the "dimensions" of

---

aims might be teaching but might equally well not be — e.g., government, a corporation, or a research institute. (Recall Newman's insistence that research science be excluded from the university and confined to institutes!) Thus, by definition, a theological school's course of study cannot be organized by any "structure of the sciences"; a course of study has to do with teaching and learning, but sciences are not defined that way.

Disciplines are pedagogical areas and thus are defined by the aims of teaching, but they are "facilitated" by the pursuit of scientific research and scholarly inquiry. A discipline amalgamates the aims of pedagogy and the aims of science. (Thus Farley's "disciplines" are roughly what von Humboldt had in mind for the University of Berlin, for which we have let *Wissenschaft* be the emblem.)

Specialty fields have evolved out of disciplines and have, in Farley's view, largely displaced disciplines in North America's research-oriented universities. They focus on subtopics in disciplines (e.g., not "North American social history" nor "economic history" but "history of canal systems"), are isolated from other specialties within the same discipline, and rely on "the paradigm of narrowed empiricism." They are institutionally reinforced by the reward system in higher education, which promotes those who publish a great deal in narrow compass, and by national "professional guilds" of academics in the same specialty fields, by which academic status and reputation are determined.

Perspectival emphases are pedagogical areas that may require scholarly work in conjunction with their teaching but are not disciplines because they lack any "abstracted regions of reality" to define their subject matter. Rather, they are defined by the distinctive perspectives that they provide on reality or on human experience as such. (Consider philosophy, religious studies, and the fine arts.)

The question about the structure and unity of a theological school's course of study is a question about the structure and unity of its *pedagogical areas*. The current fragmentation of the course of study in theological schools is partly the result of identifying pedagogical areas with "disciplines" and then substituting "specialty areas" for the disciplines. Some pedagogical areas are not "disciplines" — e.g., philosophical theology (it is a "perspectival emphasis"). And some pedagogical areas are now defined by aggregates of "specialty areas" ("New Testament" becomes "synoptic Gospel," "Pauline," or "pastoral epistle" studies).

faith-within-its-situations requiring interpretation will show that "five elemental types of interpretation" are called for (*Fragility*, 141). Three are brought into life situations by faith. They are the types of interpretation involved, respectively, in grasping or thematizing "the total Christian mythos" (interpreting the tradition), in assessing the truth of the vision conveyed by the mythos (interpreting the truth of the gospel), and in engaging in faith's praxis (interpreting action). Because dimensions of faith are always interrelated in concrete actuality, these three types of interpretation are always "interrelationally copresent" (139). Two additional types of interpretation are syntheses of these three: the fourth "elemental" type of interpretation is the type required to interpret faith's situation as such; the fifth is a "special instance" of the fourth (148) — namely, the type of interpretation needed to interpret a *believer's* "primary occupation" or vocation, which constitutes the believer's own unique "enduring life situation" (141).

Each of these five "elemental types" of interpretation constitutes a "basic part of the structure of theological study." If the aim is to discipline and rigorize each of them, then each requires two things: first, each requires "knowledge of the area of concern," and second, each "makes use of whatever sciences and scholarly resources are necessary for the disciplining of that mode of interpretation" (*Fragility*, 173). This means that paideia toward *theologia* involves a *movement* back and forth, from attention to acquiring knowledge of a relevant area of concern to attention to disciplining the types of interpretation involved in acquiring that knowledge.[13]

13. Actually, a second movement takes place *among* the three elemental modes of interpretation (interpretation of tradition, truth, and action) when the modes of interpretation are themselves the focus of attention. This second movement is a move to synthesize them into two more elemental modes of interpretation: interpretation of inclusive situations and interpretation of vocations. A "situation

On the one hand, this requires what Farley calls "foundational studies . . . areas of knowledge and cognitive postures that the student needs in order to interpret tradition and action" (145). Though judgments about which particular areas fit this description will necessarily vary from school to school, Farley holds that three general areas of foundational studies are needed by any program of theological study: (1) the cultural context of religion and church; (2) philosophical understanding of the human condition; and (3) Christianity historically understood (cf. 144-47). Study of each of these areas needs to be rigorous and disciplined. Hence these foundational studies themselves appropriate relevant sciences and scholarly inquiries.

On the other hand, since each of these foundational studies involves sophisticated skill in the three types of interpretation appropriate to tradition, truth, and action, it is necessary to shift attention to the acts of interpretation themselves. In order to make students' practice of interpretation more self-consciously disciplined, it is necessary to focus on the methods and presup-

---

is a temporal-spatial configuration of . . . the surrounding world as it is experienced." It has "its own distinctive features, which are not so much 'objects' as dimensions of realities" (*Fragility*, 156). (Consider the situation of "attending the theater," for example, which has a past, a physical setting, a power structure, a set of expectations and attitudes, etc.) Interpretation of inclusive situations focuses on identifiable recurring features of such situations. Farley suggests that it is "in part a formal, perhaps even an ontological, undertaking," but as an exercise in "theology of culture" must also attend to how those recurring features are exhibited in concrete contexts of persons' lives (157). A special instance of inclusive situations is a vocation (148). Hence a fifth elemental mode of interpretation is interpretation of one's vocation, which involves a synthesis of the first three elemental modes of interpretation. Hence, in its focus on disciplining the capacities required for interpretation, theological schooling as paideia will in this second movement also focus on capacities needed for interpreting inclusive situations and vocations. It is the latter that warrants a focus in theological schooling on the roles of professional church leadership, not in order to equip future leaders with professional skills, but to school them in capacities for interpretation of themselves as leaders.

positions of relevant sciences and types of scholarship. Furthermore, on Farley's analysis, when attention focuses on acts of interpretation themselves, it is also necessary to focus on ways in which the first three types of interpretation (of tradition, truth, and action) are synthesized to comprise the remaining two types (interpretation of the situation as such, and, as a special case of that, interpretation of vocation).[14]

Note how Farley's proposal negotiates between "Athens" and "Berlin" as models of excellent schooling. Theological education is paideia aiming to cultivate a *habitus*. Like all paideia, it works indirectly by focusing study on a subject matter. In this case the subject matter is faith, and the study involves dialectical activity, central to which is the disciplining of acts of interpretation of the subject matter. Both the study of the several dimensions of the subject matter and the disciplining of interpretative skills must necessarily enlist various sciences and scholarly researches. That is, because the paideia aims at something *(theologia)* that not only has the character of *habitus* but also has the character of dialectical activity, it must embrace *Wissenschaft*. Because the *Wissenschaft* is in the service of the cultivation of a *habitus,* it is not done for its own sake. By being appropriated *into* paideia, *Wissenschaft* ceases to define theological schooling. Indeed, by being appropriated into paideia, *Wissenschaft* regains the possibility of its own reunification. As we saw, on Farley's analysis *Wissenschaft* is inherently tragic, obliged to pursue knowledge by methods of abstraction that systematically distort its objects of knowledge. This distortion can only be overcome by the countermovement of synoptic perspectives that offer syntheses of the results of the several distinct abstractive "sciences." Such perspectives have been marginalized in the modern academy. By being appropriated into the paideia aimed at *theologia,* however, *Wissenschaft* has one such synoptic

14. Cf. *Fragility,* pp. 155-62.

perspective restored to it, and with it at least the possibility of a corrective to its own disarray.

Interpretation as the Task of Church Leadership

Thus far Farley's discussion has concerned the structure and unity of theological education as such, regardless of its matrix. The discussion applies to a theological school, but with a specific modification. The modification is dictated by the matrix of "church leadership." Here there is a remarkable turn in Farley's argument. Having forcefully exposed the "clergy paradigm" as a major cause of the fragmentation of theological education, and having vigorously rejected the notion that clergy functions should specify the purpose and structure of theological schooling, Farley still finds a way to acknowledge that church leadership may indeed shape theological education. This is possible because, on his analysis, church leadership and *theologia* intersect at the point of *interpretation*. The arguments of the two books converge to make this point.

In his book *Theologia,* Farley proposes that the central task of church leadership, lay or ordained, is "the mobilization of the ecclesial community . . . to theological understanding at the service of the believers' ministries" (176). Incidentally, this is remarkably like H. Richard Niebuhr's (neo-orthodox!) picture of the proximate goal of the minister as "pastoral director." However, where Niebuhr characterized the ultimate goal of both leader and community as the increase of love of God and neighbor, Farley characterizes the ultimate goal as "redemption." The ultimate purpose of the community is to be a "redemptive community." Because the ecclesial community is a community of redemption, because believers' ministries serve redemption, and because redemption occurs in connection "with the particular mythos and 'gospel' of that community" (176), *interpretation* of that gospel is essential to the church leader's task of evoking, disciplining, and broadening believers' theological understanding. Thus analysis of the task that is central to the matrix of church leadership can yield "criteria" for the aims of specifically clergy education (180): presumably it should discipline future leaders' interpretive capacities *in such a way* that they are capacitated to empower other believers for their ministries.

In *The Fragility of Knowledge* Farley moves to the same conclusion through analysis of vocation as a dimension of faith-within-its-situation. One's "vocation" is a special case of one's "situation"; it is one's "primary occupation." For most people it is distinct from any "occupation" they might also have in church. However, for clergy "primary occupation" and "occupation in church" coincide. For them, the type of interpretation called for by vocation is identical with the type called for by church leadership. Hence it is not an arbitrary and extraneous imposition to introduce church leadership as a dimension of faith that is a subject of interpretation and a subordinate part of theological study.

The type of interpretation that needs to be disciplined here is a synthesis: "*all* of the elemental interpretive modes must collaborate in disciplining the reflective interpretations of the ordained leader and in developing the leader's required skills" (*Fragility*, 161). This has a retroactive effect, as it were, on the entire movement of theological study. The type of interpretation demanded by *this* vocation requires a distinctive shaping of the foundational studies and a correlative disciplining of the other types of interpretation. It is not that additional foundational studies are called for or that other types of interpretation are needed. The task of church leadership determines neither the subject matter nor the unity of theological schooling; its power to fragment the course of study is neutralized. It requires only that the movement between foundational studies and the disciplining of various types of interpretation be synthesized in ways specifically appropriate to the task of church leadership.

Farley's reformulation of paideia is as instructive as was New-man's. His modifications of the paideia model are designed to give a structure to schooling that can appropriate the best of *Wissenschaft* and provide a built-in impetus to critique ideological distortion, to give a unity to schooling that can nonetheless be adequate to authentic pluralisms in both subject matter and student popula-tion, and to leave room for focus on the education of church leadership without ceasing to be genuinely theological schooling.

The relative modesty of Farley's overall proposals about the *structure* of the theological course of study is clear, but it needs to be made explicit. Theological study must be "ordered learning," whether it takes place in church, seminary, or department of religious studies (cf. *Fragility,* chaps. 4 and 5). "The five herme-neutic modes [or 'elemental types of interpretation'] do not en-force a specific curriculum. . . . They provide us with certain guiding criteria but do not dictate the structure of the study itself." Indeed, Farley does "not think it is possible logically to derive a pedagogical structure from these requisites or criteria. The aims of a school's program of studies always reflect the specific situation and context of the school. In addition, any subject matter will set requirements of pedagogy that do not flow simply from the aims of study" (143) — that is, from the disciplining of inter-pretation. He is not proposing the abandonment of the classic fourfold *pattern* to organize courses, for it "did embody something of the natural movement of theological study, from concern with 'normative' historical reality to concern with truth and practice. But the fourfold pattern is only a formal apparatus and can be a framework for very different approaches to theological study" (104).

Nor, emphatically, is he urging the abandonment of "disci-plines." To the contrary, he notes that his proposal might require the development of some new scholarly disciplines. In particular he mentions "the hermeneutic description of situations as such.

If teaching in this area were developed, it would add a dimension to and perhaps redefine practical theology" (*Fragility,* 174-75). It is by this inclusion of the "disciplines," old and new, that theological schooling on a revised paideia model must include *Wissenschaft* precisely in order to be excellent paideia. Furthermore, the inclusion of these sciences and scholarly inquiries guarantees that intrinsic to this paideia is the cultivation of the intellectual capacities needed in order to detect and critique ideological corruptions of the schooling. In that way the relative naivete of Newman's version of paideia is corrected. Rather than excluding disciplines, Farley's proposal requires that the self-definitions of the disciplines used in a theological course of study not be permitted to define the divisions and overall structure of the course of study. Instead, he urges that the disciplines be organized "along lines that yield an understanding of the *dimensions* [in contrast to the historical epochs and subspecialties they generate] of the historical Christian faith" (174).

Further, his proposal requires that the movement of the course of study not be seen "as linear travel through the existing disciplines" (*Fragility,* 144). He does not even seem to want the movement between foundational studies and hermeneutical studies to be a linear movement.

This modesty about any claims concerning structures inherent in theological schooling is instructive. Instead of urging any overall structure and movement to a theological course of study, he seems finally to be urging a movement *within* all subunits of the curriculum, no matter in what sequence they come — a movement from implicit to explicit attention to acts of interpretation themselves, a movement toward self-consciously disciplined hermeneutic. That, after all, is what permits the study of any subject matter facilitated by some science or scholarly research to be truly "theological," for "theological study is, in the broad sense of the word, hermeneutic study" (*Fragility,* 173).

Farley's claims about the *unity* of a theological course of study are more robust. As for Newman, so here, the singularity of the *aim* of the course of study can unify the course of study no matter how diverse its subject matters or how various the disciplines it employs. The aim in this case is to discipline the elemental types of interpretation involved in faith's dialectical activity, moving from unreflective insightfulness to critically reflective insightfulness. The unifying aim of this paideia is demanded by the very nature of *theologia*. It is an aim relative to a single subject matter, which is, properly speaking, faith-within-its-situation. Because faith has five quite different dimensions, the subject matter of paideia falls into several parts, each requiring a type of interpretation appropriate to it. Any one of these pedagogical areas in turn (such as biblical studies, for example) "may bring together several disciplines — distinguishable pedagogical, scholarly undertakings — yet may be unified by the aim to thematize and rigorize one of the modes of interpretation" (*Fragility*, 173).

What holds the variety of the pedagogical areas and the disciplines they appropriate together as an integral whole is the fact that they are rooted in the diversity of the dimensions of a single reality, faith. Precisely the same thing may allow this unity to be adequate to the plurality of types of social location of students. For this one reality, faith, is variously shaped in the various "situations" of believers as such, and the one dialectic of faith *(theologia)* is variously shaped by the different matrices in which it occurs. By this move Farley effectively avoids the peculiarly abstract picture of schooling that Newman gave and its blindness to the pluralizing effect of the actual internal power arrangement and external socioeconomic location of any school.

Since all of this is said of theological study regardless of its social setting, it must also be said of theological study in the particular matrix of church leadership — that is, theological study specifically in a theological school. The special requirements of the functions and tasks of church leadership provide neither the unifying aim nor the subject matter of this study. The education of church leadership, too, is paideia in *theologia,* the subject matter of which consists of the several dimensions of faith-within-its-situations, and the aim of which is to discipline the modes of interpretation required by each of those dimensions. However, one of those dimensions is vocation, and church leadership may be such a vocation. As a specialized vocation, church leadership calls for its own type of interpretation. That interpretation can yield criteria by which the paideia of church leaders may be shaped. Those criteria are not an alien and extraneous imposition on theological study; they are rooted in its own proper unifying aim to discipline its elemental modes of interpretation (in particular, interpretation of vocation). Thus the essential nature of the vocation of church leadership may properly shape a theological school's course of study, as one matrix of theological study, without being the basis either of its proper subject matter or of its unity.

Critique

While there is much to be learned from Farley's proposals about how to analyze and diagnose malaise in theological schooling, these proposals also yield some cautionary morals. Doubts about the internal coherence of the project begin to rise when one asks two questions about Farley's description of *theologia* as a *habitus:* (1) Why is *theologia* both a *habitus* and a dialectical activity? and (2) Just how seriously does the proposal take the historicity of this *habitus* on which it verbally lays such stress? Two things are at stake here: the basis of unity in theological schooling and the thesis that there is a "structure" proper to a theological course of study just because it is theological.

Why is *theologia* both a *habitus* and a dialectical activity? One answer we have been given so far is largely strategic: if theology is going to be understood properly not as a body of theory about God to be applied to life situations but as wisdom in living, it needs to be understood as a disposition, a *habitus;* and if it is going to be understood as aware of its own plural settings and critical of the idolatrous and ideological distortions they introduce, it needs to be a dialectical activity made rigorous by appropriation of various types of *Wissenschaft.* Furthermore, *habitus* and dialectical activity need to be seen as two aspects of a single reality if the fragmentation of theological schooling is to be overcome. Its unity lies in its being ordered to a single goal, the cultivation of *theologia;* if that turns out to be two different things, the schooling has two goals and is fragmented again.

Have *habitus* and "dialectic" really been shown to be two aspects of a single integral reality? It is not at all clear that they have. *Habitus* and dialectical activity belong to two disparate rhetorics, each associated with a quite different view of human being. *Habitus* historically belongs with a classical view of human beings as both "characters" and "having character." That is, we are "characters" filling socially defined roles who interact in complex ways in a public realm. In doing so, each enacts her own intentions in a manner shaped by her own "character" — that is, by certain settled dispositions or *habitus* to act thus. Recall that in ancient Athens' picture of paideia, the central dispositions to be nurtured were moral virtues, dispositions to public *bodily* action of certain sorts; in Newman's revision of paideia, the central disposition to be nurtured was an intellectual virtue, a disposition to engage publicly or privately in *mental* acts in a certain way — that is, with good judgment.

Dialectical activity, on the other hand, historically belongs to a modern view of human being as subjectivity or center of consciousness. Consciousness is always consciousness *of* something. That means that consciousness is always situated within a realm of objects of which it is aware. Moreover, it is always intersubjective — that is, it is constituted by its consciousness of other subjects. Consciousness of something always involves interpretation, and interpretations always employ some set of symbols or some language. Hence consciousness is always "mediated" by language and other symbols. Furthermore, consciousness may have any of several degrees of self-awareness *in* its mediated intersubjectivity and consciousness of an objective world, ranging from "unconsciousness" to rigorous self-scrutiny. Dialectical activity constitutes the most exquisitely and rigorously self-critical degree of awareness, facilitated by all available techniques of cultural analysis, social analysis, and psychoanalysis.[15]

In short, whereas a *habitus* is a disposition to *do* something, dialectical activity is a way of being self-aware. It may be that these two rhetorics can be synthesized. Has Farley shown that they can be synthesized? Or has he simply laid them side by side because, for other reasons, both need to be affirmed to *theologia?* If the latter is true, then *both* of them become goals of theological schooling, and the basis of that schooling's unity in a single goal is lost.

Just how does Farley understand the relation between these two? This is not clear. An emblem of this unclarity is the striking fact that for all of his use of the term, Farley never says what *theologia* is a *habitus* for, what it disposes us *to.* Consider three possible ways in which *habitus* and dialectical activity might be related.

15. To be sure, Plato represents Socrates as teaching by a dialectical method intended to evoke insight regarding one's own ignorance and to evoke vision of the Good. Thereby Socrates' paideia "shaped" persons. So too both ancient and medieval philosophers labored to develop dialectic as a procedure to test the rigor and validity of arguments. However, Farley means more than this by "critical thinking."

One pattern might be this: the dialectical activity results in shaping us with a *habitus* for wisdom. We saw that this pattern was suggested by the way in which Farley first introduced the distinction between them. We have also noted that the *habitus* and wisdom are frequently linked. In that case, the *habitus* is a disposition to be wise about self, neighbor, and world in relation to God. It is a disposition always to act wisely in these regards, whether in public or in private acts, in bodily or in mental acts. Interpreted in this way, Farley's proposal presupposes a classical view of human beings as characters in roles and as having character. But if this is the pattern, it is confusing to identify *theologia* with both a process and a result. Better to restrict *theologia* to the *habitus,* and identify the dialectical activity with the paideia that evokes and nurtures the *habitus.*

But this won't work. Thus far "wisdom" has remained a vague notion. However, no matter what wisdom's precise meaning, there is no reason to believe that the dialectical activity that Farley analyzed in four steps or "moments" would yield a disposition to act *wisely.* What his analysis did show is that the dialectical activity constitutes a mode of *consciousness* that is critically very self-aware in interpreting things. This critically self-aware interpretive activity can be disciplined by appropriating various *Wissenschaften.* There is plenty of evidence, however, that persons whose consciousness has been disciplined to an exquisite level of critical self-awareness in interpretive activity are not necessarily thereby disposed to act wisely. Conversely, it is dubious that wisdom, on any definition, inherently involves this four-moment critical activity. If *theologia* is going to include awareness of pluralism and rigorous critique of idolatry and ideological distortion, it will have to be more than simply a *habitus* for wisdom whose paideia is the dialectical activity; it will also have to be characterized by dialectical activity itself. However, unless the two are somehow synthesized in *theologia,* it is simply a name arbitrarily assigned to two goals of paideia. And then the unity of theological schooling is threatened.

This suggests a second possible pattern: perhaps *theologia* as dialectical activity is what theological paideia aims to evoke and nurture, and the *habitus* is simply a disposition to engage in the dialectical activity. In that case dialectical activity is not the same thing as theological paideia (as in the first possible pattern of relationship between *habitus* and dialectical activity); rather, the dialectical activity is the *goal* of the *paideia*. That is to say that the goal of theological paideia is the cultivation of a particular mode of consciousness or inwardness. Interpreted in this way, Farley's proposal presupposes a less classical, more modern view of human beings as centers of consciousness or "subjects."

This interpretation is strongly suggested by the fact that Farley's discussion of the movement and structure of theological study focuses exclusively on the four moments of the dialectic. The aim of theological paideia is repeatedly said to be the cultivation and disciplining of the types of interpretation that make up the moments of the dialectic. (There are five types of interpretation, but the fifth is simply a special case of the fourth, so the number of moments in dialectical activity reduces to four.) For its part, *theologia* as *habitus* is introduced to block the picture of theological schooling as a movement from theory to application: no, *theologia* is not a theory that could then be applied; it is a disposition to wisdom. Once that point is made, *habitus* effectively drops out of the discussion. Perhaps, then, the *habitus* is nothing but the disposition to engage in the dialectical activity. And what paideia aims at is both to cultivate this disposition in us and to evoke practice of the dialectical activity by us.

However, this pattern also will not work as a construal of Farley's discussion. For according to this pattern, the stress on *theologia* as wisdom in regard to God is entirely lost. On this pattern, if the *habitus* is wisdom at all, it is wisdom in regard to, precisely, the four-moment dialectical activity; it is a disposition to engage in that dialectic at every opportunity. The dialectic, furthermore, is entirely formal. It is a matter of relentlessly testing theological notions for misplaced absolutes and probing for ideological distortions. It is a mode of consciousness, one way of being a subject. As dialectic it generates no normative content, no wisdom of its own. If the relation between *habitus* and dialectical activity were understood on this second pattern, theological schooling would indeed be unified by having a single goal (the dialectical activity); but it is hard to see what would be "theological" about it.

There is a third possible pattern, and it invokes a third term: perhaps *theologia* is both *habitus* and dialectical activity, not because either one entails or generates the other, but because both are rooted in something deeper, faith-within-its-situations. As we have seen, for Farley faith is a way of being in the world that is inherently cognitive. It is a kind of insightfulness or wisdom about self, neighbor, and world in relation to God that is evoked by Christianity's distinctive bundle of symbols, myths, doctrines, and actions and that is always situated in some concrete social, cultural, and historical setting. Moreover, faith is a dynamic insightfulness. The dynamic consists of faith's drive to turn its initially unreflective insightfulness into reflective insightfulness. Theological paideia is the way in which that transition is nurtured.

The very way in which faith is explained here seems to require a view of human being as center of consciousness, with faith being a possible type of consciousness and *theologia* being the name for that type of consciousness insofar as it has reached a particularly exquisite degree of self-awareness. Inasmuch as faith is wisdom in an unreflective mode, *theologia* must be that same wisdom in a reflective mode — a *habitus*. Inasmuch as faith is evoked by, but is not the same as, the "total Christian mythos," in becoming reflective it must be critically wary of confusing the culturally and historically conditioned elements of that mythos with wisdom concerning God. Furthermore, insofar as faith is always situated, in becoming reflective it must be critically wary of ways in which its cultural and historical situation may ideologically distort its wisdom concerning God. Hence, inasmuch as faith in its unreflectiveness is both culturally situated and evoked by a historical mythos, its reflective *theologia* must be rigorously and self-consciously self-critical. It must be a dialectical activity.

Faith thus seems to be a distinctive type of consciousness that always, in every time and place, has the selfsame structure; it is not to be confused either with that which evokes it (the Christian mythos) or with its situation. Faith's structure is determinate enough to dictate a structure to theological study. Different aspects of its structure require that faith become reflective and that its reflective mode be, respectively, both a *habitus* and a dialectical activity. *Habitus* and dialectical activity are independent of each other. Dialectical activity doesn't generate the *habitus,* as the first pattern had it. Nor is the *habitus* a disposition to engage in the dialectic, as the second pattern had it. Both characterize *theologia* only because each of them is required by a different aspect of underlying faith.

It isn't clear that this third way of construing Farley's proposal is coherent either. It looks as though the rhetoric that goes with a classical view of human beings as agents in a public realm has been subsumed within a rhetoric that goes with a more modern view of human beings as subjects, centers of consciousness. *Habitus* belongs with the first; "faith," "critical reflectiveness," and "dialectical activity" belong with the second. There is nothing inherently wrong with this mixing of rhetorics, of course. Philosophers and theologians have been doing it for centuries. When it is done, however, the new meaning of the concept taken out of its original conceptual home and employed in a new conceptual home needs to be clarified. In this discussion *habitus* finally remains murky. What is it a disposition precisely to *do?* Is *habitus* really coherent with "dialectical activity"? That isn't clear.

What is at stake, of course, is the unity of theological schooling. *Theologia* is the goal that is supposed to unify the schooling. *Theologia* must be characterized as both *habitus* and dialectical activity, not because either implies the other, but because both are required by the essential structure of faith. However, since dialectical activity and *habitus* are independent of each other and since the notion of *habitus* is vague, the question arises whether they finally amount to two relatively independent goals of theological schooling, both required by faith, but whose congruence with each other is unclear. In that case, theological schooling may have two goals, and its unity is at risk.

Moreover, Farley's way of negotiating between paideia and *Wissenschaft* as models of excellent schooling is jeopardized. *Theologia* requires paideia inasmuch as it is a *habitus,* and it requires *Wissenschaft* inasmuch as it is a dialectical activity. The compatibility of the two depends on the interrelatedness and coherence of *habitus* and dialectical activity. If they are quite independent of each other, and if it is unclear whether they really are congruent with one another, then it is unclear that they can synthesize paideia and *Wissenschaft* in the service of *theologia.*

The picture of faith as something that has a universal, perhaps essential, structure raises a second type of question about Farley's project. Despite the considerable stress the proposal lays on the historicity and relativity of faith and its *theologia* and the paideia that nurtures that *theologia,* just how seriously does the proposal really take historicity?

There can be no doubt about Farley's intent to stress the historical conditionedness and relativity of faith in its situatedness and to stress the implications of that for our understanding of theology and of theological schooling. Recall the evidence we have already seen.

In *Theologia* it is stressed that faith is "the way in which the human being lives in and toward God and the world under the impact of redemption" (156) and that it is always located in some concrete social and cultural situation that "varies from believer to believer, culture to culture, epoch to epoch" (157). Indeed, the *theologia* to which faith moves must have the character of a dialectical act precisely because faith's various situations constantly threaten to corrupt it. The dialectic is faith's critical self-scrutiny to protect against that corruption. So too, the paideia through which faith moves to *theologia* has several different modes precisely because it is relative to the concrete social setting in which it takes place (the situation of the believer as such, or the role of church leadership, or the academy).

In *The Fragility of Knowledge* it is stressed that the very way in which we think about faith and theology and theological schooling underwent a sea change in the Enlightenment from which there is no turning back: "Enlightenment means a shift in . . . ways of knowing. . . . According to the new cognitive posture, everything that presents itself for understanding and inquiry is part of a larger system or process of relations and events, and cognition and understanding are enjoined to go as far as evidence permits in grasping things in their relations, backgrounds, and historical and natural causalities" (91). Consequently, for example, one cannot study "religion" by positing an unconditioned "religion behind the religions" (72). This means that there is neither an actuality nor an ideality that is an entity, an essence, a universal structure, or an archetype to be the referent of the term *religion.*

Farley characteristically refers to Christian faith as a particular type of religion. Somewhat confusingly, Farley does go on to add that one aim of religious studies is "to illumine religiousness itself, religion as an aspect of human existence" (*Fragility*, 73). (If there is no "religion as such," can there be "religiousness as such"?) Whatever the difference may be between postulating an "essence" of religion and postulating "religiousness itself," presumably the reasons for rejecting the idea of an essence of religion would also require us to reject the idea of an essence of one specific type of religion, say, Christian faith. These reasons are the "relationality," the cultural and historical "relativity" of religious practices, myths and symbols, beliefs and institutions. Accordingly, the stress on historical and cultural conditionedness yields not only an acknowledgment but an insistence on the *pluralism* of Christian faith, of the *theologia* to which it moves, and of the paideia by which faith gets to *theologia*. However, if that insistence were taken with utmost seriousness, how could it be argued that there is *a* universal, situation-invariant structure to theological study? A structure of what, rooted in what?

Perhaps the answer lies in counterevidence that Farley's proposal does not finally take historical and cultural relativism with utmost seriousness. To begin with, there is a striking one-sidedness in the picture of faith's relationship to its situation. Consistently, the situation is presented as the source of possible corruptions of faith against which faith must protect itself by critical self-scrutiny. Never is the situation presented as positively constitutive of the concrete reality of faith. It is as though faith were a reality necessarily set into some situation, almost inescapably distorted by some features of the situation; but no features of the situation enter into faith's constitution to make it precisely *this* concrete instance of faith. It is as though faith has a self-identity that somehow is more basic than and is privileged over its modifications by various situations.

This sense is reinforced by the way in which the *theologia* to which faith moves is consistently characterized as a *habitus,* one more or less determinate disposition. To be sure, *theologia* is said to come in different modes, each a modification imposed by a different matrix. The differences among these modes turn up, apparently, in *theologia* as "dialectical activity." Each matrix imposes different concrete content to the four moments of the dialectic. One looks in vain, however, for ways in which different matrices modify *theologia* as *habitus*. *Theologia* seems to be one selfsame *habitus* in all matrices. But if faith is aptly described as "the way in which the human being lives in and toward God and the world under the impact of redemption" (*Theologia*, 156), why should not faith's *theologia* embrace a number of *habitus*, each a disposition to "live" in a different way "under the impact of redemption." They would be different dispositions partly because redemption "impacts" us in complex ways evoking a range of dispositions, and partly because what counts as the dispositions for living appropriately "under the impact of redemption" varies concretely from situation to situation. If historical and cultural relativity were taken with deep seriousness, *theologia* as *habitus* would be relativized and plural. Instead, it appears to be the case that while the historicity and pluralism of *theologia* may be acknowledged at one level, underneath it *theologia* as *habitus* universally maintains a single invariant self-identity.

Similarly, for all the announced irreversibility of the Enlightenment's discovery of the conditionedness and relativity of all "realities," the study of theology is said to have a single invariant "structure." Theological study has five areas, which are dictated by the structure of the study's object, faith-within-its-situations. That object is said to be a reality with five "dimensions," each of which can be abstracted from the concrete whole and attended to by one of the areas of theological study. The general thrust of the argument is clear: Although its historicity means that the actual material content of theological study may vary from culture to culture and from epoch to epoch, the formal structure of theological study is universal and invariant because its object, faith-within-its-situations, has a structure that is universal and unmodified by its historical and cultural settings. A self-identical reality seems to be posited underlying all historical and cultural relativities in theological study.

Moreover, in this case it is clearer what gives faith and theological study (and perhaps *habitus,* too?) their invariant, universal self-identity. It is a structure. The phrase "self-identity through diverse situations" simply points to a reality; it does not entail any particular theory about why the reality is the way it is. However, the claim that theological study has a structure *and* that it is grounded in the structure of the object of that study — namely, faith-within-its-situations — does seem to entail a theory about the self-identity-through-change of faith, theological study, and so forth: the self-identity is rooted in a structure that is not itself conditioned by or relative to culture or history.

What sort of structure is this? Perhaps the answer is suggested by Farley's apparently odd remark that while there is no such thing as an "essence" of religion, there is such a thing as "religiousness itself." He goes on to characterize it as "religion as an aspect of human existence" (*Fragility,* 72-73). Elsewhere in *The Fragility of Knowledge* he takes up the same theme:

> The personal-individual aspect of religion (of *religiousness*) originates in the strange way in which the human being is self-conscious about its own deepest problem and situatedness. The human being exists in the world . . . in self-conscious anxiety about the meaning of its experience and destiny. Its most fundamental striving or desires . . . move past or through its worldly environment and thus occur on an infinite horizon. When the human being responds to what it construes that infinite horizon to be (God, Atman, nature, being, sacred powers), *this anthropological structure generates religiousness or piety.* (61-62; emphasis added)

The structure in question is a structure of "human being" or "human existence." More exactly, it is rooted in the structure of human consciousness and self-consciousness. Within this structure, the content of consciousness is culturally conditioned and historically thoroughly relative. Indeed, it may be this very structure that makes it possible for us to "transcend" that historicity enough to be conscious of it. However, apparently this structure is not itself culturally and historically relative. This is, of course, that more modern view of human being we noted earlier, to whose rhetoric belong such terms as *dialectical activity* and *critical reflectiveness,* and to which *habitus* is an alien term. The structure of consciousness is universal in human consciousness, self-identical and invariant.[16] This structure is not to be confused with the "essence" in which, as we saw, Newman roots the unity of a university's course of study. Newman grounded the unity of schooling in the universal and invariant structure of reason objectively considered. It was a cosmic principle, the principle of order and intelligibility of all that is insofar as it is real. By contrast, the structure on which Farley grounds the self-identity of "religiousness itself" is the structure, not of reason as such, but of distinctively human consciousness; it is the structure not of the cosmos but of subjects.

Now Christian faith is, for Farley, a specific type of religiousness. This explains the type of self-identity he ascribes to faith and the sort of unity he seeks for theological schooling, but it threatens his proposal's capacity to acknowledge and cope with deep, irreducible pluralism in theological schooling. As a type of religiousness, faith has a structure rooted in the structure of human consciousness. Since the structure of consciousness is ahistorical, so the structure of faith will be self-identical through

16. We are further encouraged to interpret Farley's writings about theological schooling and theological study along these lines by his careful and rigorous exploration of just this anthropological structure in *Ecclesial Reflection* (Philadelphia: Fortress Press, 1982).

all cultural and historical changes. So too, the underlying self-identity of *theologia* as *habitus* and of theological study are rooted in the same structure. By the same token, pluralism in theological schooling must be viewed as reducible to modifications on a basic theme rather than as finally in some way irreducible.

I suggested earlier that Farley's proposals seem to ascribe to the "Christian thing" the type of unity that belongs to a distinctive way of being "set" into the world and the distinctive perspectives on the world that that affords. And we have seen repeatedly that he stresses the reality of pluralism in theological schooling, both a pluralism of construals of the "Christian thing" and a pluralism of socioeconomic worlds from which students come and into which they go. Left at that, there would seem to be no tension between the affirmation of pluralism in theological schooling and Farley's proposal about how to regain unity in theological schooling.

If, however, the unity of faith as a way of being "set" into the world is ultimately grounded in the ahistorical structure of consciousness of the *subject* who is "set" into the world, then pluralism must be looked at in a particular way. Now the pluralism of construals of the Christian faith cannot be seen, radically, as fundamentally different if overlapping construals. Rather, this pluralism must be seen as modifications of a single invariant structure — a structure, furthermore, that we can locate and describe. And a pluralism of social worlds must be seen as a series of variations on a single underlying theme, the structure of human consciousness as such. This has the advantage that it gives some precision to the concept of pluralism, which more often than not is used with stupefying vagueness. It leaves one wondering, however, whether it does justice to the depth of the historicity of social "reality," including the "Christian thing."

Pluralism with Unity in Accord with "Athens": The Mud Flower Collective

If we focus on the realities of cultural pluralism as we analyze what is wrong with theological schooling and ask what is theological about it, we get a very different picture of the enterprise. I noted at the beginning of this chapter that in addition to discussions like Farley's of issues raised by the loss of unity in theological schooling, the current conversation also includes discussion of issues raised by the realities of cultural pluralism both within and outside theological schooling. If the first type of discussion suggests that theological schooling is fragmented because it is inadequate to the ideal unity of its subject matter (e.g., for Farley, "faith-within-its-situations"), the second type of discussion suggests that theological schooling is inadequate to the reality of plural construals of the "Christian thing" and to the reality of cultural pluralism, both within theological schools and in the world into which their graduates go to offer churchly leadership.

The most elaborated instance of the second type of discussion is the Mud Flower Collective's *God's Fierce Whimsy*. The Collective consisted of seven theological educators: Katie G. Cannon, Beverly W. Harrison, Carter Heyward, Ada Maria Isasi-Diaz, Bess B. Johnson, Mary D. Pellauer, and Nancy D. Richardson. The members of this group of women themselves differed in regard to race, ethnicity, class, and sexuality. They were all "based professionally in the Northeast" in association with schools that are "commonly held to be on the progressive edge of liberal Protestant thought and practice" and therefore were very conscious of not being able to speak "universally about women's experiences in Christian seminaries."[17] Nonetheless, they did re-

---

17. *God's Fierce Whimsy*, p. 7; subsequent citations will be given parenthetically in the text.

gard themselves as "a typical theological body, representative of all theological educators and students" with respect to the ways in which as a body they were "fragmented by the diversity of our cultures, our experiences, and our commitments" (63).

Several features of this book are striking: its clarity about the limits of its goals, its remarkable integrity, and its candor. The Collective was clear from the outset that the book was intended to pioneer a new way of discussing theological schooling and so could hope to be "only a starting point, a spring board into further discussion" (203).

The book's integrity has to do with that "new way" of discussing theological schooling theologically. For reasons we shall explore, the Collective was committed to the view that theology must be done as concretely as possible. The way to do that, in their view, is to keep it as closely tied as possible to persons' lives and experience. In this case, it is tied to the lives of the Collective's members and to their experience in working together. They determined that this book must not only commend such a method but must also be an instance of it — that it must not only "say it" but also "show it." That determined the movement and style of the book. It has far less abstract expository writing and far more concrete writing — in the form of dialogue, letters, poetry, and ritual language — than theological books usually do. Together, they re-present to the reader the movement and structure of the Collective's experience in working its way to theological insight about theological schooling. That gives the book a remarkable integrity that commands respect.

That integrity leads to candor about the tensions the members of the Collective experienced in their work together and about the limits of the outcome of their work. Among the limits, they expressly acknowledge not having adequately come to terms with racism, sexism, homophobia, classism, motherhood, and the nature of writing and language (cf. 197-202). The candor about tensions intersects with candor about limits. "Yet we confess that we are puzzled, even as our 'product' goes to press, about what the concrete implications of Mud Flower's relational difficulties may be for theological education" (202). The intersection is important because it underscores this: if we stress that theological schooling must be adequate to theological and cultural pluralisms that cannot be reduced to variations on themes, then we must insist that a theological school embrace conflicts that we know in advance may not be resolved by the applications of any body of theory.

Misplaced Universalizing

On the Collective's analysis, theological schooling is currently inadequate to the irreducible pluralism of types of human experience defined by race, class, and gender. In particular, the Collective stresses the effects of the exclusion of women's experience: "Christian seminaries are in serious trouble, having failed, by and large, to appropriate either the meaning and value of women's lives or the intellectual/professional offering of women and men who bring a feminist commitment to theological education" (145). They make it clear throughout the book that "women's experience" is itself no one thing but rather is pluralized by race, ethnicity, and class.

This diagnosis has a conceptual corollary that is a major thesis of the book. Theological schooling's inadequacy to genuine pluralism correlates with its reliance on what we might call "misplaced universalizing." The standard way to do theology

> is to assess the nature and character of universals, to sweep with broad strokes the particularities of personal and specific events; to bypass the nitty-gritty pains and problems, whims and fantasies, of the common folk in an effort to direct us away from ourselves toward that which cannot be known in human experience. (64)

It will not do to object to this by saying that it assumes simplistic and incoherent views of knowledge and of language according to which all we can know or speak about are concrete particulars, for the Collective assumes no such thing. To the contrary, they universalize often, never more vigorously than when polemicizing against the hegemony of "white male experience." That certainly looks like a universal. It can be debated whether there actually is such a thing as white male experience. It can be debated whether the universalizing method described above is caused by white male theologians regarding "only their own experience as normative in making Christian doctrine" and insisting that everybody else do the same (64; cf. 44), or whether there are other causes. But it can hardly be debated that the phrase names a "universal." And the Collective need not be read as polemicizing against "universalizing" as such. They do not advocate a "theory" on this subject. Rather, the Collective is objecting to theologians "universalizing" in the wrong *place* — namely, in trying to understand what God is and how to know God, and in making claims about what human being is and how we know.

The key to correcting theological schooling's inadequacy to genuine pluralism lies in making it properly theological. And the key to making it properly theological lies, according to the Collective, in doing theology in a fashion "that is foundationally oriented toward justice and that is relational in character. To do theology ourselves we must begin with our experience of ourselves in relation" (141). This is to be done in a collaboration that includes a diversity of cultures, in accountability to very particular people — "black and Hispanic women and those white women who are struggling against racial, sexual, and economic injustice" — who are committed to transforming theological schooling so that their needs and interests "are realized as basic to the methods and content of the enterprise," by "beginning with our own lives-in-relation. We believe that this is where all research, teaching, and learning should begin" (24; cf. 23-27).

The way to do this concretely in theology is to begin with

the stories of the persons engaged in this collaborative enterprise: "If there is anything worth calling theology, it is listening to people's stories" (134; cf. 209). There are at least three reasons for doing this. The first reason is that such listening allows theological reflection to focus on relationships. The basic theological convictions are (1) that God is known as God is experienced and (2) that God is experienced in relationships. People vary a great deal regarding the types of relationship in which God is experienced. If we attend especially to the imagery people use in telling their stories, we may identify which types of relationship have been the occasion for experience of God that shaped their understanding of God. The Collective does not develop this point theoretically. Instead, it devotes a chapter to sections of the stories each member told of her own life, and the reader sees the point emerging from the stories: God is experienced as present or as absent in relationships with a mother or a father; in relationships, both positive and negative, with persons who are ethnically or racially "other"; in relationships with fellow activists in a movement seeking justice.

A second reason for beginning theological reflection with people's stories is that this quickly exhibits ways in which those lives have been victimized by injustice. We need not fear that to begin theology by hearing people's stories is to privatize theology, focusing it primarily on persons' subjectivities or interior lives. To the contrary, "the personal is political" (156). Persons' stories quickly exhibit the need "to be the subject of our own stories." Indeed, the need for that is "one of the few things" the Collective is "confident in speaking of as a universal" (99). Persons' stories also quickly exhibit ways in which that need is systematically thwarted by "structures of evil," arrangements of power that unjustly privilege some at the expense of others. Furthermore, as they are heard by others in a collaborative undertaking, people's stories may exhibit ways in which they are complicit in those unjust power arrangements, helping — however unintentionally and unconsciously — to deform others' efforts to be the subjects of their own lives (89). The ways in which persons are subject to and complicit in these structures of evil are highly particular and can be seen in their diversity only by attending to their differing stories. Thus to begin theology by hearing other people's stories not only keeps theology "relational in character" but also keeps it "foundationally oriented toward justice."

The third reason for beginning theological reflection with people's stories is that this keeps the focus on relationality and on justice as concrete as possible. Stories, of course, are highly concrete forms of communication. The images in the stories on which we are especially to focus are also concrete. The fact that the stories can be told and heard in a collaborative setting that includes cultural diversity means that the stories overlap enough to be understood across lines of "otherness" that divide the listeners. They are publicly intelligible. The fact that the stories are concretely diverse will block premature and misplaced universalizing about "common human experience," "faith," and "human nature" as ways to explain their public character. This generates a new set of criteria of adequacy for theology. Theological work has been understood

> to proceed in deductive or analytic modes of thought; the primary value of theological reflection to the reader or student appears to be clarity, coherence, precision, universalizability of abstraction, and order. Theological adequacy is measured by these characteristics and also by conformity to one's theological tradition. These criteria have their place, but when enabling people to do theology in a constructive fashion is a genuine concern [as it presumably is in a theological school], such criteria must be understood as, at best, provisional, and as subsidiary to other values. (157-58; cf. 91)

The concreteness advocated for theological work here dictates a different set of criteria of adequacy for theology: "perceptiveness, insight, depth and breadth of critical illumination, and respect for the diversity of experiences of persons in different social locations" (158).

If this is how "doing theology" is best understood, then this has implications for theological education that aims at enabling people to do theology constructively. There is an instructive, if formal, parallel here with Farley's project: for Farley, if you want to overcome theological education's fragmentation you must get straight what "theology" is; for the Mud Flower Collective, if you want to overcome theological education's inadequacy to genuine pluralism you must likewise get straight what "theology" is. Both, furthermore, lead to the adoption of a variation of "Athens" as a type of excellent education. For the Mud Flower Collective, too, theological education shapes persons as persons (cf. 142). It aims to bring them, as did the Collective's own common experience, to greater self-knowledge, including (in excellent Socratic fashion) consciousness of ignorance.[18] In particular, theological education should shape people so that they are capable of being the subjects of their own lives, lives whose relationships may be occasions to experience and understand God and whose praxis is oriented toward establishing justice. Since God cannot be understood directly, this theological paideia, like all others, accomplishes its goals indirectly — in this case by focusing on people's stories and the relationships recounted in them. Furthermore, as has always been the case when theological education has the character of paideia, this paideia creates a specific social space, for "community grows in our acting together on behalf of our common need to be taken seriously as the subjects of our own lives. . . . In the biblical tradition, this solidarity is called love" (100).

However, in important respects the Collective's version of

18. Cf. *God's Fierce Whimsy*, pp. 197-203, and the outline of the pedagogical implications of the Collective's work, pp. 204-5.

paideia differs profoundly from both Newman's and Farley's. The difference lies in the Collective's deep skepticism regarding claims about the universal essence of "human nature" or "reason" or "Christian faith." This has particularly instructive consequences for a picture of theological education.

For one thing, this type of paideia requires a community that is inclusive of genuine diversity-in-unity. The Collective seems mostly to assume the unity. Although the book makes almost no reference to it, the ground of that unity would appear to be the fact that what all participants experience in their particular and disparate relationships is *God*. The diversity comes from the fact that different types of experience, different groups of experiencers, are rooted in different social, economic, and political locations. That means that differences in types of experience of God are irreducible to some common denominator such as "the structure of human consciousness." They are not mere variations on a theme, although they may overlap in varying ways, allowing mutual understanding and public communication. The mark of their being "genuinely" pluralistic is this irreducibility.

The Collective's stress on inclusiveness is emphatic. They characterize their discussion of theological schooling as "feminist" theology for two reasons. One, of course, is their own commitment to the particular experience of women. The other is their desire "to call theological educators to a professional mandate: to examine how power is experienced in human life and how it is structured in the methods and content of what is taught and learned in seminaries" (13). They are emphatic, however, that they do not exclude men, even white men, or their experience. Only one thing may be excluded: "There is no room in theological education for refusal to engage in dialogue, for closed minds, for shut-down hearts. There is no room for indifference to human well being" (152). Accordingly, one mark of excellence in theological schooling is that its paideia takes place in a community inclusive "in its faculty and student body" of "increasing numbers of women of different racial/ethnic groups as well as racial/ethnic men" (153).

The inclusiveness required by the paideia of excellent theological schooling, on this model, leads to a second instructive implication for the nature of theological education. The fact that the different groups of persons making up a genuine pluralism have different social locations means that they are differentiated in large part by their varying degrees of social, economic, and political power. The differences among them are not only differences in types of experience of God; they are also differences in experiences of justice. In the view of the Collective this makes justice issues central in theological schooling. In its final summary of the implications of its discussions for theological schooling, the Collective begins with this assertion: "The fundamental goal of theological education must be the doing of justice" (204).

Does this mean that justice issues have displaced God, or "the intellectual love of God" (H. Richard Niebuhr), or "faith's prereflective insightfulness under the impact of redemption" (Farley) as the overarching goal of theological education? Possibly, but probably not. The Collective's point seems rather to be that concern for justice lies at the heart of an intellectual love of God and neighbor, at the heart of faith's situation-within-the-world. Justice issues are not merely an implication of love of God and neighbor. They are not merely a corrective of ideological distortions of faith's insightfulness. They are the heart of the matter. The argument might go like this: If relationship with God (love of God; faith's insightfulness) is experienced in personal relationships, then care of the former mandates care of the latter. And if personal relationships are relationships between persons with different social power, then care for the former mandates concern about the justice of the latter. Therefore care for people's experience of God mandates above all attention to justice issues. This bears on a theological school in two ways. On the one hand, it means that no schooling or research may be done that is indifferent to the issues of justice it raises (cf. 204). On the other hand, it means that the school as a whole must devise mechanisms by which the power arrangements within its common life are kept under critical review regarding their justice (cf. 12).

A third implication regarding excellence in theological education is that there is no single ideal structure to the course of study in such a school, and certainly no one best curriculum. Negatively it can be claimed that to date the experience and social location of one group (relatively affluent white males) has exercised hegemony over theological schooling. As one of the members of the Collective wrote in a letter, "Those in power tend to render things 'universal' in a cloning fashion or else tend to define their worth, value and quality out of existence by assessing them as liabilities and inferior" (44). The Collective's summary of the implications of its conversations for theological schools' curricula is that this hegemony of one group's experience must stop. Hence "cultural pluralism is critical in the attempt to examine the value of what is taught and what is learned" (204).

Positively, however, each school must work out the structure of its course of study in the light of its particular purposes, particular history, and present situation. The only universal constraint is that it involve a community inclusive of genuine pluralism and that its central goal be justice. This too is instructive. If a theological education's adequacy to "genuine" (i.e., irreducible) pluralism rules out postulation of some one universal, ahistorical, "essential" structure to "human nature" or "reason" or "human consciousness," then by the same token there is nothing to dictate a universal, ahistorical structure to theological study or to a theological school's course of study.

A final consequence of this version of paideia for theological education has to do with its unity. Theological education adequate to "genuine" pluralism will have a type of unity that not only expects but invites internal tension and conflict. This is an inescapable corollary of adequacy to deep pluralism both within a school and within the school's host society. The Collective made this the central point of their concluding recapitulation of their analysis:

> Real education and spiritual growth occur only where it is impossible to avoid the conflicts and tensions that rend our world and the lives of each of us. The difficulties we have encountered in probing our brokenness, even in spite of existing bonds of trust, should stand as a sobering reminder of the meaning of what we propose. (203)

Tension rather than harmony is the sign of health in theological education on this view. Indeed, prolonged harmony would be an early warning signal that something is amiss.

It is not that on this model of excellence in theological schooling unity is a matter of indifference. No institutionalized enterprise could survive indifference to unity. Rather, the *type* of unity it envisions is quite different from that assumed in classical paideia.

Classical paideia and the versions of it we have seen in Newman and Farley all ground their unity in a goal to nurture or cultivate something that has a universal structure ("human nature," "reason," *theologia*). The internal coherence of that structure guarantees that the schooling itself will be harmonious *in principle*. That does not rule out conflicts generated by differences of opinion and clashes of personality. However, it does promise to *contain* those conflicts and to provide a resolution of them through the thoughtful application of underlying principles universal to all. The fact that the unifying goal of these versions of paideia has a structure that is universal means that it is also "transcendental." That is, it is not itself ever located in any one particular concrete reality. The structure is not the sort of thing that could ever itself be a (relatively powerful) contestant in conflicts and clashes. Rather, it is the context that is necessary for the very possibility for opinions to conflict and personalities to clash. It defines the field of combat and "transcends" them all.

The version of paideia adopted by the Mud Flower Collective, however, entails a rejection of any such postulated structure. On their proposal, to be sure, theological schooling's unity is rooted in a goal: the goal of shaping persons so that they may become the subjects of their own lives, capable of experiencing God in and through their relationships. But that goal may not be said to have a universal structure. "Personal lives" and "experiences of God" are concrete and particular. They doubtless overlap in various ways, or they could not be publicly understood. However, the goal of theological paideia can be characterized adequately without commitment to any claim about some one structure shaped universally among them all. These lives are each a center of power. They have various social locations and belong to various groups of persons, each of which is itself a center of social, economic, and political power. They are a pluralism of powers. Insofar as that power is distributed unjustly, there will be conflict among them.

Thus, insofar as persons' experiences are shaped by different social locations, differences among them regarding experience of God in particular will generate tension. Without any structure universal to all these groups, there is no "transcendental" framework to contain tensions and promise ultimate resolution of conflicts. What then will hold this pluralism together as a diversity-in-unity? For the Mud Flower Collective, in theological schooling the diversity will be held together, it seems, by a commitment to the pluralism that is freely embraced by all parties. It is a commitment to a method: to listen and to speak to one another precisely as powers genuinely *other than* one another.

Theological controversy is no longer guaranteed any ultimate resolution by virtue of the coherence of the transcendental structure of the controversy's subject matter. Theological education can no longer be guaranteed a structure rooted in a universal structure that transcends the powers that conflict as actual people actually engage in inquiry. Theory as theological reflection and praxis as engagement in tensions and conflict among centers of power can no longer be supposed to be separable. Rather, theological reflection consists of plural centers of power genuinely listening and speaking to one another *as* "other." Such theological education would ideally have the unity of a vigorous ongoing, multi-party, tension-ridden conversation, not the unity of a harmonious structure.

Critique

The instructive consequences of this type of excellent theological education bring their own worrisome features. Two in particular grow out of what the Collective did *not* discuss, and a third grows out of things they did write. The first of these concerns has to do with what the word *God* means in this discussion, and it raises questions about the relationship between language and experience. As we have seen, the Mud Flower Collective's proposal lays a great deal of weight on the conviction that women commonly experience God in relationships, a claim that is more assumed than argued. One does not need to be committed to a strong view of God's transcendence over us and our lives to feel the need in some way to distinguish between experience of God and experience of a relationship. Otherwise "God" and "experience of God" begin to look like alternative names for "relationship" and "experience of a relationship." Although it is clear that the Collective has no interest in "reducing" God to human relationships, what is needed is precisely one of the things that they acknowledge

147

is missing in this book: sustained reflection on religious and theological language.

Providing that reflection would seem to involve taking stands on controversial *theoretical* issues about how language works so as to be intelligible. In particular it would involve taking a stand on the controversial question of whether concepts emerge out of prereflective experience or whether all experience, including prereflective experience, involves something like concepts. Here the question would take this form: Do people prereflectively experience God in their relationships and then subsequently find more or less adequate ways to express it conceptually? Or are the experiences they have of God shaped from the outset by the culturally and historically conditioned concepts they bring to the experiences? If the former is the case, then we can take people's stories about relationships in which they experience God straightforwardly. If the latter is the case, however, then we may not be able to treat those stories as innocent starting points for doing theology; we may need to subject even those stories to critical assessment of possible ideological and idolatrous distortions imposed by their cultural and historical relativity. Clearly, what is at stake here is the methodology that this proposal argues makes theology properly theological: starting with people's stories about their lives.

A second concern has to do with the picture of paideia as inclusive, collaborative conversation. Does it include adequate grounds for self-critique? It is precisely the proposal's stress on historically and culturally relative pluralism that underscores the importance of this question. Such relativity, we have seen, leads groups to use religiously sanctioned ideas and values to obscure and rationalize their own unjust privileges, and it leads them to idolatrous confusion of commitment to partial insights with commitments to ultimate truth. In a theological education that is adequate to genuine pluralism precisely because it includes the pluralism in an ongoing conversation, what are the bases of critique of the ideology and idolatry that each group may bring into the conversation? To be sure, each group can be counted on to raise critical questions about the perspectives and commitments of the other, but is that sufficient? Idols conversationally added together do not necessarily overcome each other's partiality, nor do they cumulatively tend to approximate ultimate truth. One ideology is not necessarily a good critique of another; more than difference of view is required for critique.

This question brings into bold relief the striking absence in this proposal of two things that could serve as additional bases for critique: the "Christian thing" and *Wissenschaft*. The proposal is strikingly silent about any construal of the "Christian thing" or, in Farley's phrase, the "total Christian mythos." Yet that mythos has often served as the basis of stringent critique of idolatries. The absence of reflection on possible roles for *Wissenschaft* in this paideia is also remarkable. It is not that the Collective polemically rejects rigorous and disciplined research. To the contrary, they insist that research as it is currently practiced must be reformed, not abandoned. However, they do not develop the point. Nor do they explore how a properly reformed *Wissenschaft* should be incorporated into the paideia they envision. They do not explicitly negotiate between Athens and Berlin. Yet *Wissenschaft* has frequently been the basis for rigorous critique of ideological distortions.

The third concern regarding this proposal arises from its deep skepticism concerning universal claims about the essence of "human nature" or "reason." The worry is this: Can such suspicion be held consistently? If not, is the proposal in danger of a deep internal incoherence? We have noted two important turns in the Collective's argument in which they themselves make or seem to make just such universal claims, once explicitly and once implicitly. The explicit claim is that as persons we "need to be the subjects of our own stories," a claim that is "one of the few things" they are "confident in speaking of as a universal" (99). Why do we have that need? And on what basis is the Collective confident of its universality? That "need," if the reasons for it and the implications of it were elaborated, would seem to entail a full-blown view of human nature that is as *universally* attributable to human beings as is the "need" from which it was elaborated.

A closely related issue is implicit in the Collective's claim that theology properly done must be "foundationally oriented toward justice and . . . [must be] relational in character" (141). We have seen that the reasons for stress on relationality lie in views about the tie between experience and knowledge of God. Where, however, do the reasons lie for making an orientation to justice "foundational"? What view of justice is at play here? More particularly (given that the question we are exploring concerns the coherence of this proposal), can the idea of justice be elaborated without drawing on some view of human nature and some view of reason that are claimed to be universal? Indeed, does the concept of justice used here rest on the concept about (universal!) human nature that makes us all "need" to be the "subjects of our own lives"? Can this entire proposal be elaborated coherently if some such moves are *not* made? Clearly, asking these questions in no way entails that the answer to them is necessarily "no." However, concerns about the very possibility of making a coherent case for this sort of modification of the "Athens" type of excellent theological education can be put to rest only by devising ways to deal with such questions.

*   *   *

In this chapter we have examined two very different proposals about the nature and purpose of excellent theological education, each of which is tied to a significantly different understanding of the nature and purpose of theology. For Farley, theology is faith's inherent insightfulness or wisdom brought to a high level of self-conscious critical reflection. For the Mud Flower Collective, theology is critical reflection on the narrative of persons' lives that attends to the concrete particularity of different persons' experiences of God and to the ways in which those same lives have been victimized by injustice.

Both proposals adopt the "Athens" model of excellent theological education. Each negotiates with "Berlin" on the home ground of "Athens," but with difficulty. One of the problems we have seen in the "Athens" type of excellent education, in all of its forms — its classical form in the ancient world, its form in the history of Christianity, and the form Newman gave it — is its failure to provide adequate bases for critique of ideological and idolatrous distortions of human understanding. Both the Collective's proposal and Farley suggest that this could be corrected by incorporating into the "Athens" type the "Berlin" type's stress on *Wissenschaft*. However, for all of the Collective's stress on the centrality of ideology critique in theological education, its proposal did not develop its way of negotiating with "Berlin" far enough for it to be clear how the academic disciplines would function within theological education conceived in a modified "Athens" way. Farley, by contrast, did develop a suggestion about how the academic disciplines might be included in theological education conceived on a modified "Athens" model. However, it was not clear that the way in which education conformed to "Athens" (education as paideia leading to *habitus*) in Farley's proposal is coherent with the way in which it was to conform to "Berlin" (education as a "dialectical activity").

Each proposal addresses a different basic issue in theological education, and does so in a way that undercuts the other's address to its chosen issue. The presupposition of Farley's solution for the unity and fragmentation issue in theological education is his view of the nature and purpose of theology. He proposes to ground the unity of theological education in the inherent unity of *theologia,* whose unity is itself grounded in the universally self-identical character of faith. In turn, faith's self-identity across lines of cultural and historical epoch is itself apparently to be explained by a view of the universal structure of persons' consciousness. The Mud Flower Collective proposes that theological education can never be made adequate to the deep pluralism in the ways in which God is experienced and known if the nature and purpose of education are premised on an underlying "universal" essence or structure, either in Christian faith or in human beings.

From the Collective's perspective it looks as though proposals about what makes theological education theological that are based, like Farley's, on such "universals" are inherently incapable of taking pluralism with full seriousness. The presupposition of the Collective's resolution of the pluralism issue in theological education is their view of the nature and purposes of theology, which rejects universalizing talk about "human being" and stresses attention to the concrete particularity of individual persons' life stories. From Farley's perspective it looks as though proposals grounded in that way are incapable of fully coherent formulation because they seem to require, and perhaps tacitly even trade on, the very sort of "universal" claim about human being that they reject. Thus what seems to underlie the differences between the ways in which these proposals address their respective central issues is a deeper difference about how to think about "human being" — that is, deep differences in philosophical anthropology.

Obviously, the questions we have raised about each of these proposals are not beyond answer; the difficulties have not been shown to be beyond conceptual repair. Advocates of either position can be expected to develop and refine it. What is of continuing importance are the deep and perhaps permanent lines of tension between these two *sorts* of proposal about what makes theological education theological. Of particular importance, as we have seen, are the tensions created by different pictures of theology and the consequences those different pictures of theology have for various matters: for the effort to address effectively *both* the "unity" issue and the "pluralism" issue; for the effort to negotiate in a *coherent* fashion between "Athens" and "Berlin"; and for the effort to specify in a *consistent* way what makes theological education theological.

5

"Berlin": Unity and Pluralism in the Current Discussion

The current discussion about what is theological about theological education focuses, I have suggested, on two broad types of issues, and in the process it offers various ways to negotiate between "Athens" and "Berlin," between paideia and *Wissenschaft* cum professional education as models of excellent education. In the previous chapter we examined two examples of ways in which that negotiation may be done on the "Athens" model's terms. Farley's analysis of what's wrong with theological education and the remedies he proposes focused, as we have seen, on issues of unity in theological education. The Mud Flower Collective, in contrast, focused on issues of pluralism in theological education. Although both proposals adopt paideia as the type of education appropriate to theological study and explicitly or implicitly urge its modification to embrace certain types of *Wissenschaft*, they disagree strongly about whether there is some transcendental structure that is self-identically, universally in all types of theological schooling, no matter where it is located.

Instead of proposing to negotiate a synthesis of "Athens" and "Berlin" on the "Athens" model's home court, as the proposals we have just examined do, a second current in the present discussion of theological schooling tries to negotiate between them on the "Berlin" model's terms. Here too, some proposals take the central issue to be theological education's adequacy to a postulated ideal unity of the "Christian thing," while others take the central issue to be theological education's adequacy to pluralism.

We shall examine an instance of each. Exemplary of the first type is *Christian Identity and Theological Education* by Joseph C. Hough, Jr., and John B. Cobb, Jr.[1] Exemplary of the second is Max L. Stackhouse's *Apologia.*[2] Although the authors of these books wrote in their own names and on their own authority, each of these studies explicitly grew out of discussions of theological education in the theological faculties to which the authors belong. Both schools, one on the west coast and the other on the east coast of the United States, are associated with mainstream liberal Protestant denominations.[3] Thus both books grew out of collaborative work analogous to that which produced *God's Fierce Whimsy,* although a much less intense and sustained collaboration.

1. Hough and Cobb, *Christian Identity and Theological Education* (Chico, CA: Scholars Press, 1985).

2. Stackhouse, *Apologia: Contextualization, Globalization, and Mission in Theological Education* (Grand Rapids: William B. Eerdmans, 1988).

3. At the time they wrote, Hough and Cobb belonged to the faculty of the Graduate School of Theology in Claremont, California (Methodist); Stackhouse is on the faculty of the Andover-Newton Theological Seminary in Massachusetts (United Church of Christ).

Unity with Pluralism in Accord with "Berlin": John B. Cobb, Jr., and Joseph C. Hough, Jr.

Cobb and Hough place their proposal clearly within the "Berlin" type — or at least half of it: "The theological school is to be understood as a *professional* school. As such, its primary purpose is the education of professional leadership for the church."[4] They appear to accept Farley's view that the central problem with theological education is its loss of unity. Furthermore, along with most of the other authors we have discussed, they too hold that the basis of restored unity lies in theological education's overarching purpose. In this case the proposal is that the overarching telos of theological education is "the aim of providing the special education appropriate to church leaders" (5). Moreover, they agree with Farley that professional church leadership cannot be properly understood in a functionalist way (93).

The congruence of this with "Berlin" is evident. Recall that the rationale for including theological schooling in the newly founded University of Berlin was precisely that it prepared professional leadership for the churches (which were necessary for society's well-being) and that such preparation was best done in conjunction with *Wissenschaft,* the best of modern scholarship. We also noted that this bipolar structure of the "Berlin" type leaves it open to serious distortion, since one pole may come to be stressed to the disadvantage or even the near exclusion of the other pole. In particular we noted that the "Berlin" type underwent modification in studies of American theological education from Kelly onward in two ways: (1) the *Wissenschaft* pole increasingly shifted from education in how to do critical research to instruction in the results of research in an ever-growing number

---

4. Hough and Cobb, p. 19, emphasis added; subsequent citations will be given parenthetically in the text.

of fields, and (2) the "professional" pole was increasingly understood in a functionalist and individualistic way. Hough and Cobb share this modification of the "Berlin" type in its tendency to play down the *Wissenschaft* pole, but they resist its tendency to understand "professional" education in functionalist terms.

They disagree with what they take to be Farley's explanation of *why* theological education is fragmented: "The current problem for the theological school is *not* that it is a 'professional' school, dominated by the 'clerical paradigm.'" Hough and Cobb propose that the problem has two other roots. The first of these is that

> the church has become uncertain and confused as to what constitutes appropriate professionalism. There can be no clear unity to theological education until there is recovery of clarity about the nature of professional leadership within the church. (5)

This confusion has left church leadership open to ideological distortion by its host culture as it "conforms to expectations established for it by a bourgeois society" (93). Later Hough and Cobb add a second cause of theological schooling's fragmentation — the tension between the two poles of the "Berlin" model itself:

> Theological education is torn between academic norms, defined chiefly as excellence in the historical disciplines, and modern professional norms defined in terms of excellence in performing the functions church leaders are expected to perform. (16-17)

This analysis sets the agenda for their discussion of theological schooling. They set out to clarify what professional church leadership is and how to reconcile "professional" education with *Wissenschaft*.

In order to clarify the nature of professional church leadership, it is necessary to be clear about the nature and purpose of the church. Here Hough and Cobb's movement of thought implicitly replicates H. Richard Niebuhr's and explicitly rejects Farley's. Farley thought that what we had to get clear first was the nature of theology, *theologia*. Hough and Cobb object that Farley's account of *theologia* "would so focus on personal and ecclesial life as to distract attention from the historical horizons of the world God loves" (4). They fear that an explanation of *theologia* in terms of persons' inescapably private inwardness and the structure of human consciousness will be unable to exhibit theology's necessary engagement in action in the public realm. Better to explain the nature of theology in terms of the church's life and mission as a community active in the public realm. Such a theological understanding of the church will dictate in turn, as it did for Niebuhr, a theological understanding of church leadership.

The Nature and Mission of the Church

A properly theological account of the church and its professional leadership must begin by placing the church in the context of God's work: "God has always and everywhere been creatively and redemptively present and working; and she is now and always will be creatively and redemptively active" (21). Consequently, the church must be considered in a world-historical context (20). For the most part, the world is unaware of God's activity. However, within the world-historical context there is a historical line beginning with the emergence of ancient Israel, who "concentrated on God's activity" (21). Hough and Cobb trace this history to the Christian churches:

> Christianity is that movement within human history in which the efficacy of Israel's witness to God's creative and redemptive work has been mediated through Jesus and the apostolic witness to God's activity in him. This witness affirms not only the activity of God in the world but also her loving forgiveness and acceptance of all those sinners for whom Jesus died, that is, all human beings. (24)

Since the church is that institutionalized community whose awareness of God's redemptive and creative activity is shaped by the story of Jesus, it is a community that is constituted by *memory* — namely, its memory of Jesus. Hough and Cobb's most frequent characterization of the nature of the church is this: "The church is the community which keeps alive the memory of Jesus Christ in the world" (49).

The Christian church *has* an identity, according to Hough and Cobb. It is constituted by the church's memory. It is best described by telling the church's story, narrating its memory: "This is who we are. We are the people to whom the following things have happened." Drawing on H. Richard Niebuhr's distinction, Hough and Cobb call this narrated memory the church's "internal history," in contrast to its "external history."

"Internal history" is the history that participating members of a community tell about themselves; in it the importance of events and their interconnections are assessed by the events' capacity to shape the community's common life and invest it with meaning. It is characteristic of narratives of "internal history" that the current generation includes stories of events happening to ancient and very alien people as part of its own story. Who we are as twentieth-century Presbyterians, for example, cannot be told by narrating only the story of American religious history; we are also the people to whom certain things happened in sixteenth-century Geneva and in tenth-century Scotland and in fourth-century Rome and in first-century Galilee and in the family of Abram of the Chaldees. "External history," by contrast, is told as though by an outside observer; in it the importance of events and their interconnections are assessed by their power to "explain" subsequent events.

That is not to say that successive narrations of the church's inner history do not change. "Although Christian identity is always determined by an internal history centering on Jesus and the apostolic witness to him, its content and valuation are continually changing" (28). For example, the narrative of some churches has come to be broadened to include the internal history of other groups. (The story of who we are as twentieth-century Presbyterians, for instance, includes the story of the Council of Trent *and* of the Second Vatican Council.) It could also be broadened to include events outside Yahwistic Judaism, for the creative and redemptive work of God can be discerned everywhere (29). For example, the event of the Enlightenment has inescapably become part of modern churches' internal history.

The authors are clear that the church can easily use its internal history in distorted, complacent, self-justifying, and idolatrous ways. Interestingly, the two illustrations the authors give of this — individualism and a dualistic view of human nature — come from the Enlightenment (cf. 31-43). Rather than necessarily signaling the authors' rejection of the Enlightenment, however, this fact may simply show the self-critical power of intellectual movements rooted in the Enlightenment. Although modern individualism and a dualistic view of human nature may have their roots in the Enlightenment, so also do the modern techniques of radical self-critique that Hough and Cobb both celebrate and use as partial antidotes to idolatry. Nonetheless, it must be admitted that, although it is now part of the church's internal history, the Enlightenment appears in this book largely as a source of dangers and distortions for the church. Although the authors stress that there need to be checks against these distortions, they are remarkably unclear about just what those checks are (cf. 27-28).

Distinctive features of the church's internal history give its communal identity a distinctive shape and define what the church's *purpose* is. Three features of that distinctive identity are notable. First, because God's activity takes place in the midst of political, economic, and social history, it takes place in institutions. Indeed, "the primary theological understanding of human institutions is that they are among the crowning creative-redemptive achievements of God" (50). Accordingly, the church cannot be just an intersubjective communion of human subjectivities. It is necessarily an institution, and its institutionality is to be valued positively.

Second, because God's activity in the world is creatively and redemptively *for* the world, the church whose identity is constituted by remembering God's activity must itself be for the world. This specifies part of the church's purpose: to be "not simply a community of caring people, but a community dedicated to mutual caring and ordering its [institutionalized] life to that end" (52). This caring includes evangelism, telling its internal history because "those who know the story's healing and directive power want others to know it too" (54). Further, this caring is to be for the *whole* world in which God acts, including the dispossessed and oppressed; and the church is also to care for the world in its intellectual and cultural fragmentedness by serving as an "integrator" (cf. 55-67).

Third, as a place of awareness of God's creative and redemptive action in the world, the church's inner life centers on worship and holiness. This is the other part of the church's purpose. On the one hand, in response to God's activity in the world, the church is brought to repentance for its failures in being "for" the world, and it commits itself to be a community "in which the practices of faith, hope, and love are habitual. . . . the community of holiness is the community within which the Christian character is both nurtured and expressed by the practice of distinctly Christian virtues — faith, hope and love" (71). On the other hand, in response to God's activity, the church engages in worship, the "practice of the community of the people of God by which they reaffirm their tradition as a living tradition, one in which God is met ever anew" (75). It is striking that although worship is described as "the central act of the church, that activity apart from which the church cannot be a church at all" (74), it is not mentioned as the church's purpose until the end of a long and somewhat disconnected list of "images" that characterize the church's distinctive identity.

Thus it is that a theocentric description of the church as a community that discerns and announces God's activity in the world yields an account of the purposes of the church that is rooted in the church's identity. In this context, theology is given a teleological definition: "The major task of theology and ethics is to encourage students to think globally as Christians about the issues of the day. To think *as Christians* is to think from the memory of the church" (105). To do theology is to think about the things the church is *doing* in and for the world out of its memory of what God has been and is doing in and for the world. The authors agree with Farley that if theological schooling is to overcome its fragmentation theology needs to be reconceived, but they worry that his way of reconceiving theology as *theologia* is so focused on personal and intra-church life that it remains disconnected from the public realm. In contrast, Hough and Cobb have defined theology by reference to the mission and common life of an institution that in its God-relatedness is inescapably located in the public realm in which it may be more or less active.

Minister as Practical Theologian

A properly theological account of professional church leadership can only be given in terms provided by this theocentric account of the nature and purpose of the church. Hough and Cobb are clear that not all church leadership is "professional." That term ought to be applied only to those who are "appointed leaders to perform certain representative functions" (77). On the other hand, "professional" church leadership is not limited to the ordained clergy. Images of professional church leadership have changed several times in North American religious history. Under the impact of recent cultural changes, the churches have become as bureaucratized as any other institutions. That generates a range of expectations of professional church leadership as "management." That sociological fact is warrant, in Hough and Cobb's judgment, for the conclusion that "the minister as Manager is the strongest candidate for the dominant image of professional leadership" (78).

Thus what makes the leadership "professional" is that it bears the marks of a manager. What are these marks? Relying on Harold Leavitt's analysis, the authors urge that excellent management "consists of *problem-solving, implementing,* and *pathfinding.*"[5] What makes the leadership "church" leadership, lay or ordained, is that it is the work of a "practical theologian." A "practical theologian" is analyzed here as a combination of "Christian thinker" and "reflective practitioner."

"Practical Christian thinkers" are "pathfinders" for the church. They are capable of helping congregations to envision goals for the church in its global context. Key to this is helping Christians to perceive their situation as Christians. This needs to be done, not by applying shared ideas, theories, or principles, but by illuminating the present by the church's internal history, by exhibiting the relevance to contemporary events of the church's memory, especially of Jesus. That involves both knowledge of the history of past efforts at the same task and knowledge of scholarly study (i.e., "external history") of the church's internal history. Such leaders need

---

5. Hough and Cobb, p. 79. The reference is to Harold J. Leavitt, "Management and Management Education," The Stockton Lecture, London Business School, 16 March 1983.

first, a clear Christian identity; second, an extensive and reflective understanding of what constitutes that identity; third, self-consciousness as to how that Christian identity shapes perception of the present concrete world-historical situation; fourth, wise discernment of the implications of this Christian perception for action. (84)

"Reflective practitioners" are "implementers" and "problem-solvers" for the church. In addition to engaging in practical *thinking*, they participate in reflective *practice*. Here Hough and Cobb join Farley in their own way to reject the picture of church leadership as a movement from theory to application. Their explanation of their alternative implicitly depends on Donald Schoen's analysis of *reflective practice*. "Practical Christian Thinkers reflect not only *about* practice. They also reflect *in* practice" (85). The church community, including the professional church leader, is already engaged in the activities that comprise its mission. The reflective practitioner is especially skilled at working collaboratively in this activity with fellow church people to identify problems in this practice, devise means of solving them, and test the means against the community's vision of its goals. The work of the reflective practitioner can even involve a type of "reflective research" that may profit from being done in an educational setting (87).

Neither the "practical Christian thinker" nor the "reflective practitioner" can be subsumed to the other; each demands the other. Together, in the authors' view, they comprise the best image for professional church leadership today — the "practical theologian." This is not a functionalist picture of church leadership:

Practical theology is not one function along with others. It is a mode of reflection that continuously reevaluates the use of time and energy in and by the church in light of what the church truly is. A shift of roles or functions [e.g., from preaching to liturgy, or from counseling to social action] would not affect its appropriateness. (92)

To be engaged in practical theology, to be a professional church leader, simply *is* to be doing theology "professionally" on Hough and Cobb's description of theology.

Theological Education as Church Leadership Training

The character of theological education follows from the nature of professional church leadership as "practical theology" since the unifying goal of theological schooling is to educate such leadership. As the theological discussion of church leadership in the context of a discussion of the nature and mission of the church shows, four things need to be provided by theological education.

First, there needs to be a "close connection between the subject matter of courses in Bible and church history and the deepening, broadening, and clarifying of Christian identity" (95). It is in the study of Bible and church history that "the church's future leaders learn who they are as Christians" (97) — that is, they learn of their "Christian identity" by learning their "internal history." Study of this internal history should be critical, to check against inaccuracy and idolatry. It should include the internal history of women and minorities in the Christian movement. It should tend toward universality because "the basic identity of leaders for the church should be as inclusive as possible. . . . The goal is that we experience our identity with all for whom Jesus died" (101). On this view, "particularism" — that is, "the particular focus on God's work with those people who have recognized it" — is something to be *"overcome"* (101; emphasis added).

Currently the effort to turn study of Bible and church history into a grasp of Christians' internal history has relied on critical "objective" history combined with hermeneutical theory applied to

166

bring out objective history's meaning for the community. This is the basis of Farley's proposal about the structure of theological study. Hough and Cobb believe that this is inadequate (cf. 97). They seem to be calling for a new range of questions to govern study of Bible and church history. Not just "what happened?" and not just "what is its meaning?" but "who does it assert that *we* are?" needs to be the question to which all aspects of the inquiry are ordered. This is not a question that sets the agenda or dictates the methods of any of the academic disciplines in intellectual or institutional Christian history, Old or New Testament. Accordingly, course work in these subject matters in theological education can no longer be defined and organized as they have been by research agendas and methods of the relevant disciplinary specializations. Here Hough and Cobb agree with Farley. Courses will, to be sure, presuppose the research of those specializations. They may well engage in some of it too. But the purpose of such courses is no longer *wissenschaftlich*, to capacitate students to go on to do such research for themselves. Despite their few occasional comments about the importance of theological schooling in these subjects being "critical," Hough and Cobb are explicit that preoccupation in such courses with "methodology" is a symptom of what's wrong with theological education today (cf. 3). Accordingly, their vision of theological education would seem to require that courses dealing with these subject matters would have to be survey courses oriented to the question "Who does this material say that we are?"

As we have seen, consciousness of Christian identity needs to be set in a global setting. Hence the second requirement of theological education of "practical theologians" is that it must generate a well-informed and highly self-conscious "global consciousness" in students.

Clearly, not every Christian will have an identical view of the most salient features of our global situation. There are many legitimate differences of judgment. But we cannot consider our internal history seriously without acknowledging that God's work is for the whole world. (103)

This can only partly be accomplished by sustained instruction; it also requires the "presence of a multiethnic, multicultural student body and faculty" (104) and student and faculty visits in third-world countries. Note that in this way Hough and Cobb address issues about the adequacy of theological schooling to pluralism precisely *by* the way they address issues about the unity of theological education.

Third, theological education of "practical theologians" needs to capacitate future church leaders as "practical Christian thinkers." In traditional terms the relevant subject matter is that of "theology and ethics." In Hough and Cobb's framework, the "major task of theology and ethics is to encourage students to think globally as Christians about the issues of the day" (105). Fulfilling this task requires a transformation of theology and ethics as they have usually been understood. To begin with, the separation between the two must be overcome. Then the "subject matter" must change: although practical Christian thinking must be a thinking "from the memory of the church," it can no longer be a thinking *about* the memory of the church, about what exemplary earlier Christians thought about their situations. Rather, it must take as its central subject matter the church's mission in the present global situation. The purpose of courses in theology and ethics, then, would not be to explore ethical "positions" or "systems" of theological thought as such but rather to "help students to become practical Christian thinkers" (106). "It is the style of thinking, not the particular conclusions, that the seminary can teach" (108).

Here too, no established academic discipline in theological education takes the church's mission as its subject matter. Contrary to present arrangements, the structure of the curriculum in regard to the need for educating practical Christian thinkers cannot be dictated by any structure or map of the sciences. Indeed, "abolition of disciplinary boundaries would be a first step toward liberating seminary faculties to consider the most important issues facing the church and to encourage students to do so as well" (107).

Finally, in dialectical relation with the third need, theological education of "practical theologians" needs to capacitate future church leaders as "reflective practitioners" in parishes. This is

> the joint task of the church and the seminary. While the church must assume a major responsibility for education for pastoral reflection in practice, the seminary makes its major contribution by providing opportunities for reflection *on* the practice of Christian leaders in general and specifically on the practice of pastors. (127)

Churches would assume the major responsibility for this if they adopted Hough and Cobb's proposal that, following graduation from theological school, students be placed in "teaching congregations" for one year as "probationary ordinands." Here in "the institutional location of pastoral practice under the supervision of practicing ministers" is the place "where church management, polity, and general pastoral care can best be taught" (121). The theological school, for its part, would assume responsibility for course work that studies Christian congregations in all their variety, as well as course work that focuses on models of practice, thus cultivating students' capacities to reflect on ministerial practice (cf. 121-25).

These are not four parts of an essential structure, nor are they four moments of a movement essential to theological schooling. They do not dictate any particular curriculum, although the authors offer a concrete example of what a curriculum that accorded with these four desiderata would look like (cf. 129-30). They are simply the four desiderata of any excellent theological education, which follow from a theologically warranted picture of professional Christian leaders as "practical theologians."

Critique

This proposal to recover the unity of theological education by negotiating between "Berlin" and "Athens," but on the "Berlin" model's terms, is both instructive and worrisome. It is particularly instructive in showing the possibility of reconceiving the unity of theological education on a teleological basis (as have the other proposals), but without postulating an ideal "essential" structure to the education's ultimate subject matter. Accepting the conventions of the "Berlin" type, it grounds the unity of education in its overarching goal of educating professional church leadership for the churches. What makes this education *theological* is that its goal is defined theologically and not functionally: it is leadership of those who share "Christian identity" — that is, that community which recognizes and responds to God's creative and saving activity in and for the world — guided by that same Christian identity. In this regard the proposal recovers the theological integrity of the "professional" education pole of the "Berlin" type from distortions in prevailing twentieth-century modifications. Theological education that is unified by having all of its aspects ordered to this one goal would also be a kind of paideia. It would be a shaping or forming of persons in their Christian identity, especially in their capacities to think about that identity practically and to practice it reflectively so that they can offer others "vision" and help in "implementation" for their common enactment of Christian identity. It incorporates the "Athens" type on the "Berlin" type's terms.

It is worrisome, however, that this proposal's way of recovering unity in theological schooling on the "Berlin" type's terms appears to be at the expense of *Wissenschaft*. The worry is not created by Hough and Cobb's critique of established academic disciplines and their boundaries. Farley, who takes *Wissenschaft* with utter seriousness, does the same. Rather, the difficulty comes with the authors' resistance to attention to "methodology" in studies of Christian identity in theological education. It is not that they fail to recognize the power of disciplined, critical research to unmask idolatry and ideology in intellectual life. They make this point themselves a couple of times, although they do not much emphasize it. Rather, the difficulty is that they do not seem to appreciate how education into the practice of disciplined critical thinking is crucial to church leaders' capacities to offer both vision and implementation in a fashion that involves genuinely perceptive assessment of the present situation and truly insightful grasp of Christian identity. Knowledgeability about the *results* of studies of the world-historical situation and about the *results* of biblical and historical studies, but not about their methods, would not be sufficient for that sort of leadership.

The deemphasizing of *Wissenschaft* is also worrisome because it threatens to undercut theological education's importance to the church. Hough and Cobb themselves make the point that, while the churches desperately need "intensive thought" about their mission in the present situation, they entirely lack the "organs for that kind of thinking." Theological education, however, "would seem to be a place for serious thought about the church's mission" (107) and thus is in a position to provide the churches a singular service. The suggestion has striking parallels with H. Richard Niebuhr's insistence that theological schools must be "intellectual centers" for the church. Furthermore, Hough and Cobb's proposal could address a problem we found with Niebuhr's proposal. Niebuhr, we saw, construed the intellectual work of theological schools entirely and explicitly as "theoretical." We worried that that left it entirely unclear how or why we should expect it to make any difference to action. The polemic against the picture of theological schooling as a movement from theory to application, which we have met in all the current literature about theological schooling, only underscores that worry. Hough and Cobb have an entirely different picture of the character of theological schools' intellectual work. It is not the task of developing a body of theory to be applied later to action. Rather, it is the reflective practitioner's reflection *about* action *while* acting. We noted in passing the authors' observation that there is a type of research that is congruent with this picture of a theological school's intellectual work; but they never elaborate. Their proposal's relative denigration of schooling in methodologically disciplined research makes it seem unlikely that the type of theological school they envision could in fact become the sort of resource of the church for which they themselves call.

It is striking, finally, that in none of this does Hough and Cobb's proposal depend on the postulation of an unhistorical structure underlying the "Christian thing." It should not be thought that "Christian identity" is just another way of naming a postulated essence of "faith" or "religiousness as such" or "reason" or "human nature." It might be, but it is not so necessarily; and in Hough and Cobb's hands it seems not to be.

To be sure, "identity" points to the same fact as "structure" does: commonality in and through change and diversity. However, there is this possible difference, which Hough and Cobb seem to be exploiting. To postulate an essential structure is to urge that commonality in diversity and change requires that, permeating or underlying all the varieties and changes, there must be some one pattern or structure that itself transcends the cultural variations and historical changes and "explains" the commonality. However, to speak of "identity-in-variety" can draw attention to a completely different way of looking at the matter. Here the suggestion is that the integrity of the historical and cultural concreteness of the lives of persons and communities must be respected above all. Correlatively, "commonalities" ought not to be reduced to some one "explanation" (the ahistorical and nonrelative "structure" of consciousness, or whatever). Rather, commonalities may be looked at as family resemblances created by innumerable overlaps of an indefinitely large number of features. There is no way to map all of that exhaustively. No exhaustive description of any one person or community is possible. However, descriptions adequate for certain purposes are entirely possible (for purposes of identification, for example, or of comparison on particular scores, or of analysis in particular respects, etc.). What is crucial is to keep the concrete individual life or community in its irreducible, historical, and relative individuality as the subject matter. And for that, "identity" is an appropriate placeholder. On this issue, if Farley's proposal about *theologia* was the thesis that got the current discussion of theological schooling started, Hough and Cobb provide the dialectical antithesis that keeps it going.

Pluralism with Unity in Accord with "Berlin": Max L. Stackhouse

Cultural and religious pluralism present the basic issues for theological schooling that most concern Max L. Stackhouse in *Apologia*. The book grew out of discussions about theological schooling within the faculty of his own theological school. It consists of reviews and critical reflection on papers prepared for that in-school discussion and on books and essays generated by the wider conversation about theological schooling. In these reflections Stackhouse gathers an agenda of issues and theses that he develops in a proposal that concludes the book.

The central theses of Stackhouse's proposal come together in this paragraph:

> The vocation of Christian theological education is to prepare women and men to be theologians and ethicists in residence and in mission among the peoples of God in the multiple contexts around the globe. The core of this preparation must be the cosmopolitan quest for the truth and justice of God. In Christian theological education, these will be best treated by careful, critical, and constructive concern for orthodoxy and praxiology, with the constant recognition that an *apologia* is necessary at every juncture.[6]

This clearly locates his proposal within the "Berlin" type of excellent education: "Theological education in seminaries prepares leaders for the churches. That is not all it does, but that is what it is designed for" (15). What makes a theological school a theological school is, as Schleiermacher argued, that it educates a professional leadership for a necessary practice. In this case the practice is necessary, not, as Schleiermacher held, for society's well-being, but for the church's well-being. More exactly, perhaps, this professional leadership is necessary for the church's global mission (cf. 49).

Therewith comes the crisis confronting theological education today. Precisely because it is global, the mission that theological schooling serves is contextualized in a variety of ways. Especially in ecumenical church circles, this has generated a high "sensitivity to pluralism" (23). There is a crisis about the adequacy of theological schooling's address to this pluralism.

However, although Stackhouse shares this judgment with the Mud Flower Collective and, marginally, with Hough and Cobb, he analyzes it entirely differently. The Mud Flower Col-

---

6. Stackhouse, p. 209; subsequent citations will be given parenthetically in the text.

lective, we saw, urged that the inadequacy lies in theological schools' failure to *incorporate* a pluralism of ways of experiencing and knowing into theological schooling in such a way as to preserve their respective integrities. Stackhouse, by contrast, urges that the inadequacy lies in the way in which theological schooling *is* incorporating the relevant pluralism. The grounds on which pluralism is being incorporated are "shaky" and create a situation in theological schooling that "is programmed for greater disarray and intensified conflict" (8).

Note what is implied here. "Conflict" on account of pluralism is a sign of something amiss for Stackhouse, whereas for the Mud Flower Collective it was a sign of health. The heart of the issues is this: Theological education, in Stackhouse's view, incorporates the relevant pluralism in a way that inescapably implies a systematic relativism about all questions of truth and justice regarding God; it implies that the "Christian thing" has no intrinsic unity or identity. Thus, for Stackhouse issues about unity and issues about pluralism in theological schooling come together. The root of the fragmentation of theological schooling lies in the way it addresses issues of pluralism; a more adequate address to pluralism would also resolve the questions about unity.

Stackhouse finds this problem repeatedly in the literature he reviews. Again and again he sees the same underlying issue, which he poses in terms of a long-standing philosophers' controversy between "realism" and "nominalism." Stackhouse explains that nominalists

> argued that all humans could really know was their own experience, and that on the basis of some apparently common features of particular experiences, those who had control of a culture could give names to — could "nominalize" — some general phenomena to organize them for the sake of what would make sense to their own experience.

By contrast, realists, "in the classical sense,"

> argued that when we spoke of things like God, or God's truth
> and justice, . . . we were speaking (always inadequately) of real,
> universal phenomena that not everyone experienced in the same
> way, but to which we were normatively subject in our thought
> and actions. . . . These phenomena could be known to be univer-
> sally valid by the deeper reaches of reason and revelation. . . .
> Knowledge of them was, in principle, accessible to all people, in
> all cultures, in all conditions of life.[7]

Theological educators who stress the historical and cultural
conditionedness of human knowing in general and of the "Christian thing" in particular emerge as "nominalists." They reject the
very possibility of identifying criteria by which to judge the
"transcontextual" or universal truth of differing historically conditioned pictures of what Christianity is and what conduct it
requires. On Stackhouse's analysis they are implicitly committed
to the position that any one view is as valid as any other. That,
in his view, is the basis on which theological education is by and
large attempting to be adequate to pluralism.

But this assumption will not do. As Stackhouse sees it, such
a view undercuts the very nature of the "Christian thing" and
subverts the entire project of theological schooling. For Stackhouse, the very idea of "contextualizing" the "Christian thing"
implies that there is something transcontextually "real" to be
inserted into various contexts. The "Christian thing" (my term,
not Stackhouse's!) involves claims about God and about justice.
Further, it is something whose truth and justice must be capable

---

7. Stackhouse, pp. 23-24. This is an extraordinary (and perhaps anachronis-
tic) use of *nominalism* according to which Edward Farley's work can be classified
as "nominalist" (cf. Stackhouse, p. 133) and, it appears, the "phenomenological"
movement in general is "nominalistic" (cf. Stackhouse, p. 26). (Husserl would have
been astonished.)

of being assessed, not just "for" some context, but in principle and universally. Stackhouse's entire argument seems to require the view that adequacy both to the ideal unity of the "Christian thing" and to the reality of pluralism requires that one be a "realist" of some sort.[8] It also seems to require rejection of the "nominalist" view that pluralism is finally irreducible. Beneath all the pluralism of experiences of God and of sociocultural locations of Christian living there must be at least a core that is transcontextual and that constitutes the authenticity of those various experiences as "Christian."

This has several implications for theological education, all of which are entailed in the distinctive twist this view gives to the school's overarching and unifying goal to educate leaders for the church.

> Ministers are first of all to be theologians and theological ethicists in residence among people of multiple contexts, equipped to preach and teach, organize and persuade, critically evaluate and defend as appropriate, and represent in cultic forms of *poesis* [making] and concrete forms of *praxis* [action] those genuinely cosmopolitan theories of God's truth and justice that can be reliably known and contextualized in every culture, society, and civilization, in the face of alternative religious, philosophical, and social orientations that are less true and less just. (165)

8. Note this statement by Stackhouse:

In other words, there is no possibility, so far as we have thus far been able to discern, for Christian theological education to proceed without . . . accepting at least a modified realist view of the nature of truth. . . . (Pp. 182-83)

However, it is not entirely clear that Stackhouse is fully committed to this proposition. Elsewhere, without objection and in apparent agreement, he cites evidence produced by Lamin Sanneh as suggesting that in fact "Christianity has never been fully satisfied with either an exclusively nominalist or an exclusively realist" position (p. 25).

The twist is this: Future leaders are to be educated specifically for the task of a "cosmopolitan" quest for the *truth* and *justice* of God. We will examine each of these three aspects in turn.

The Truth of God

The quest for the "truth of God" implies that theological education must focus specifically on the quest for "right" theology, for orthodoxy. There is some ambiguity about exactly what this means. It is clear that, for Stackhouse, theology is a form of *Wissenschaft*. It is also clear that theology is a theoretical undertaking, as it had been for H. Richard Niebuhr, and that theory precedes action. Stackhouse defines theology as

> the ordered discipline rooted in reliable knowledge of that which is ultimately and universally real (God), although different from both material reality and human invention, and accessible to reasoned discourse *(logos)*. Unless theology in this sense is possible, theological education is impossible and ought to be given up. (162-63)

More specifically, theology is rigorous philosophical-theological work. Its subject matter comprises doctrines, theories about God. To be sure, doctrines are stated in highly symbolic language that "points to" and "grasps" ultimate reality rather than descriptively "corresponding" to it. Furthermore, that language is culturally shaped and has changed over time (cf. 168-70). Moreover, doctrines themselves are not static; they, too, develop over time. Nevertheless, it is theology's task so to test these theories for truth that the results will be genuinely *scientia,* well-founded theoretical knowledge. This corresponds exactly to Schleiermacher's picture of how professional theological schooling in the University of Berlin would also be *wissenschaftlich.*

What is not entirely clear is whether Stackhouse is claiming

178

that we must assume the *possibility* of probative weighing of theological theories and of meaningful disagreements about them, or whether he is claiming that such probing has *in fact* been accomplished and that the disagreements have *in fact* been resolved in ways that no reasonable person could deny, and that somebody knows what the results are. The latter is suggested by Stackhouse's contention that he can identify four core doctrines that, under varying historical formulations, "have been accepted by the whole church over its entire history" and "provide the boundaries of what it means to be Christian": (1) that humanity is sinful and in need of salvation; (2) that revelation takes place in history in the way that the Bible authoritatively indicates; (3) that the doctrine of the Trinity accurately points to God; and (4) that Jesus is the Christ (170). According to Stackhouse, these are the four fundamentals of Christianity.

This is a very large claim. Unless it is circular (e.g., "If a group does not accept one of these, it doesn't count as part of the 'church'"), it raises the vexed question of whether it is in fact historically true that all four of these doctrines have been accepted by the *whole* church over its *entire* history, and how we would know.

The question "How would we know?" underlines the vagueness of Stackhouse's formulation of these four "doctrines." What is their material content? On that subject there has been and continues to be unended disagreement *within* the church. Lacking clarity about their content, how could we judge whether in fact the church accepted them in all times and places?

However, there is evidence in the book that Stackhouse has the more modest claim in view. A number of times he makes the point that theological education makes no sense unless we *assume* that it is possible to make truth claims about God and that it is possible to subject them to significant disagreement and reasoned evaluation. To assume these things does not require us also to assume that the disagreements can be *decisively* resolved, once and for all, let alone that they ever will be in this world. It does not require us to deny the possibility of reasonable disagreement not only outside the church but within it as well. All that would be claimed is this: *If* we engage in the practice of theological education, *then* we commit ourselves to the view that it is *possible* to make truth claims about God and to weigh arguments in favor of and against them, even if they never are and perhaps never can be "knock down" decisive arguments. Perhaps this is the force of Stackhouse's contention that theological education must focus on "orthodoxy": it must not focus on those *theories* about God certified once and for all to be "right" or true, but instead must focus on the ongoing *task* of testing our theories about God to get them as "straight" or as "right" *(orthos)* as we can. At any rate, that would seem to be all that he needs to urge in support of his analysis and critique of theological schooling.

The Justice of God

The quest for the "justice of God" implies that theological education must focus on what Stackhouse calls "praxiology," the assessment of "right action" of Christian *praxis*.

> The distinctive function of theological education in this area is one of interpreting, learning, and teaching *how theory and practice are related* and ought to be related through the clarification of that kind of justice which can, and ought to, guide *praxis*. (187; emphasis added)

(I will try later to show that there seems to be a tension within Stackhouse's discussion of theory's relation to practice.)

Stackhouse is clear that Christianity does not "involve any specific orthopraxy [right action] at all" (184). A theological school is not in the business of "prescribing 'right actions' for the world." Instead, theological education in this area consists of shaping "the will, the heart, which is the mainspring of practical action for justice in the world" (187). This is the point at which Stackhouse's proposal includes a type of paideia within a form of education that basically adheres to the "Berlin" type of excellent theological schooling. Here tensions between "Berlin" and "Athens" are negotiated on the "Berlin" model's terms.

Stackhouse's proposal can be read to urge that theological education must shape the will by a paideia that forms in students dispositions to "right action," to Christian *praxis*.[9] The "basis" of this *praxis* is a piety structured by institutions, policy, and principle. The piety "includes at least prayer, worship, and mission" (190). For Christians, piety is given structure by the institutions of baptism and the Eucharist and by the polity governing ministry. Piety is further structured by the policy it adopts regarding its relation to its host society: Will piety "resist the social and cultural patterns of its civilizational environment" or will it "recognize structures in the social and cultural environment with which it can work . . . ?" (196). Each choice structures piety in a distinctive way.

Piety is also structured, finally, by moral principle. Institution and policy must be tested as to their justice. This must be done in a "deprovincialized" way, in full consciousness of the global context in which *praxis* is enacted. Stackhouse argues that justice can be assessed by transcontextual principles: for example, that "the law of life is love" (204); that the goal or *telos* of human life is defined by the *telos* of God's action — namely, justice, for which the Christian "symbol" is "the Kingdom of God"; and that "internal to the *praxis* of God's justice is an eternal moral law" (207). Theological education as paideia shapes us to be disposed to engage in this piety structured in these three specific ways. This involves cultivating, not only dispositions for Christian

9. For this paragraph, cf. Stackhouse, pp. 190-208.

praxis, but also our capacities for reflecting upon our *praxis* so that it is genuinely principled activity. And *that* requires our engagement in rigorous, theoretical, *wissenschaftlich* inquiry in moral theology.

Here a curious tension appears in Stackhouse's account of theological schooling as focused on "praxiology." The function of theological education in this area is to explore "how theory and practice are related" in Christian *praxis.* How are they related? Stackhouse's discussion seems to entail two quite different views that are not easily synthesized.

When theological schooling's focus on "praxiology" is construed as a type of paideia (as it mostly seems to be throughout the book's eleventh chapter, "Praxiology?"), the relation between theory and practice is treated in very much the same way Hough and Cobb treated it. The paideia seems to be aimed at making us "reflective practitioners." Rather than capacitating us to be skilled at moving from theory to application in practice, or from theory to assessment of action after practice is over, the schooling seems to be aimed at capacitating us for principled reflection upon our Christian *praxis* while we are engaged in it.

However, when theological education's focus is on "orthodoxy," the relation between theory and practice seems to be treated as though it were precisely what the first view rejects. Now "doing theology" seems to be an engagement in a *wissenschaftlich* theoretical undertaking that logically must come before practice and be applied to practice. It is not self-evident that these two views of the relation between theory and practice are coherent, but Stackhouse has not explored the matter.

Cosmopolitan Theories of God's Truth and Justice

Finally, the quest for "cosmopolitan theories" of God's truth and justice implies that the core of theological education is *apologia* of a distinctive type. *Apologia* means "making a case for" or "demonstrating the truth of" doctrines. Repeatedly in Stackhouse's discussion of the quest for God's truth or "orthodoxy" and the quest for God's justice or "praxiology" we have seen him stress "that an *apologia* is necessary at every juncture" (209). Apparently he thinks that this is necessary because orthodoxy and praxiology are two sides of a single enterprise of which *apologia* is the center: "*Apologia. . .*, marked by a quest for orthodoxy and praxiology, must become the core of theological education" (208).

In Stackhouse's view this *apologia* has a definite agenda. It must show that religion is not "a derivative or epiphenomenal expression of something else — something more fundamental, more objective" (142) — but rather that it is

> based on a fundamental presupposition that there is a metaphysical-moral realm that is real, transcendent to the empirical world, and simultaneously sufficiently present to human reflection and experience that it can be taken as the decisive point of reference for the understanding and guidance of empirical life and historical existence. (143)

It must show that religions make a difference in human life. It must show that some religious claims are less true or less just than others. The global context of the church's mission requires *apologia* to be done in a distinctive way. It must be *cosmopolitan*. That is, it must take the realities of worldwide cultural and especially religious pluralism more seriously into account than earlier types of *apologia* did (cf. 159-60).

Accordingly, whatever else it may be, if theological education "is not a center for the formation of the mind through academic training, it will have failed in its primary task" (141). That task can be specified more exactly: it is to capacitate students' minds quite specifically for apologetics, for making well-warranted cases for theories about what can and cannot be known about God, what should and should not be done in fidelity to God's nature and action. Theological education should capacitate students to *demonstrate* universally and transcontextually what is God's truth and justice.

If the overarching goal of theological education is to educate future professional leadership for the church by capacitating them for *apologia,* marked by a quest for orthodoxy and praxiology, how does that goal affect a theological course of study? It does not imply any particular structure of movement for the study of theology. When Stackhouse discusses the "fields" in the curriculum, he simply assumes without argument the validity of Schleiermacher's three-part curriculum; it is not clear what his rationale for this structure is.

The first part of this three-part curriculum consists of historical fields, which Schleiermacher called "historical theology." Stackhouse locates biblical studies, world religions, and church history in this section. Incidentally, just why any of them should be included in theological schooling is not explained. If biblical studies is included because of one of the four core "doctrines" that Stackhouse says the church has held everywhere at all times (namely, that God is revealed in history in the ways to which Scripture testifies), then it is odd that world religions and church history are included in the same field. There is no similar "core doctrine" that says that either of them testifies to God's self-revelation. The basis for inclusion of world religions and church history in theological schooling would have to be quite different. The second part of the curriculum consists of normative fields, which Schleiermacher called "philosophical theology." These embrace systematics, ethics, and missiology. And the third part of the curriculum consists of the practical fields, which Schleiermacher called "practical theology." This includes preaching, education, church management, psychology, and pastoral care.

While the focus on *apologia* with regard to the truth and justice of God does not imply any change in this structure, it does imply a distinctive orientation for all courses in each of these fields. The way Stackhouse works this out is instructive. It is as though the academic work done in each field must be guided by a distinctive overarching or, we might say, "horizon" question. Thus historical scholars can contribute to *apologia* by

> testing the adequacy of what they do [not merely by meeting standard historical-critical standards for historical research, but beyond that] by showing how it aids in clarifying God's truth and justice in new and wider contexts. If these studies fail the test, they will properly be relegated to antiquarian hobbies. (219)

Accordingly, course work in the historical fields must basically be governed by this question: What in these historical materials is pertinent "for contexts around the globe"? Stackhouse suggests that biblical scholars, for example, working within the horizon of this question, would order their research and teaching to answering these questions: Is there anything in these texts that is "of universal and perennial import for knowing God's truth and justice"? Anything that is pertinent "only to contexts that are structurally, functionally, and semiotically similar to the contexts in which these texts appeared and to which they speak"? Anything that is pertinent "only to the contexts in which they first appeared"? (218).

Stackhouse calls historical work governed by these questions "postcritical theological reflection about the meaning of a text" (218). Does his view assume the validity of a distinction in a historical source between its possibly universally true "kernel" and its historically conditioned and limited "husk," with the implied promise that we can extract the more or less widely pertinent kernel from its time-bound husk? If so, it would be strikingly like the fundamental presupposition of much of late

nineteenth- and early twentieth-century "liberal" theological ex-
egesis of Scripture. This was precisely the way of seeking wider
pertinence of ancient writings that fell into disrepute because it
drew an arbitrary and unwarranted line between what is and
what cannot be "conditioned" by its historical setting. Though
there is nothing wrong in seeking texts' wider pertinency, the
liberal way of doing it increasingly came to seem so incoherent
that any attempt to resuscitate it would require careful argument.
Surely its revival cannot be accomplished simply by asserting
that it is valid after all.

Course work in the normative fields contributes to *apologia*
by clarifying "the means by which metaphysical principles of truth
and moral principles of justice can be known with relative relia-
bility" (219). The work of the normative fields is, as Schleiermacher said, basically philosophical work. Accordingly, course
work in the normative fields must be governed by this question:
What can be shown by well-warranted arguments to be universally true and just? This requires of such work the willingness to
take the risk of proposing normative answers, of presenting "models of orthodoxy and praxiology" and defending them (220).

Course work in the practical fields contributes to *apologia*
by adjudicating "the adequacy of what the others offer." Those
in the practical fields accomplish this adjudication by testing
against "the psychological disabilities, the power plays and hidden
interests, the structural constrictions, and the stinginess and
meanness that preoccupies much of life in every context" — in
short, by encounter with "sin, and the need for salvation."
Furthermore, they must do this testing in the widest possible
context — that is, in a global context. Apparently course work in
the practical fields should be governed by some such question as
this: Can these theories be applied in these contexts in ways that
bring salvation to the modes of sin encountered here? Stackhouse
says that the practical fields "are, in some senses, at the mercy of

the historical and the normative thinkers, for they inevitably rely on understandings of the past and on proposals about what is true and just in what they do" (220).

It falls to the practical fields to make the move from theory to application. Once again the strong contrast between Stackhouse's proposals and the others we have examined in the current discussion is confirmed. The others agree that the roots of the disarray in theological education today lie in large part in its implicit assumption that theological education is a movement *from* theory *to* application; then, in their different ways, the other proposals seek to replace that assumption with some other picture of theological education's inherent movement. In contrast, Stackhouse's proposal, in making *apologia* central (and also in its "orthodoxy" pole — though apparently not in its "praxiology" pole), seems to continue to assume the validity of the theory-to-application picture of the movement of theological education.

The centrality of *apologia* in this proposal highlights a curious internal incongruence throughout the book. Clearly the author has a high estimate of our rational capacities. Indeed, the final chapter begins with a section called "In Praise of Reason." Much of the argument of the book would seem to require the claim that "reason" has a single, ahistorical, and transcultural "nature" or "essence" in all human beings. However, the book itself does not venture into a theoretical discussion of the concept of "reason." This book has, rather, the character of a prophetic warning. It seeks to call theological educators back from the abyss of intellectual and moral relativism and the vacuousness and triviality that they entail. It can be safely assumed that none of the parties to the conversation would, on reflection, deliberately adopt a position of thoroughgoing theoretical relativism. Nonetheless, on Stackhouse's analysis, theological educators drift toward relativism when they attempt to address pluralism (in itself an important thing to do), but in misguided ways. What is misguided about these attempts, Stackhouse seems consistently to say, is that (however unintentionally) they imply that Christianity cannot make rational truth claims or, if it does, that there are no rational criteria by which they may be assessed. According to what concept of "reason" and "rationality"? Obviously, the answer is *Stackhouse's* concept of reason, although this concept is not much explained. The failure to explain or give reasons for that concept of reason suggests that Stackhouse assumes it to be self-evidently the concept to which everyone is accountable; if it is self-evident, it needn't be reasoned.

However, it does not appear that the thinkers about whom Stackhouse is worried are adopting their responses to pluralism simply out of a high "sensitivity" to pluralism. They seem to have adopted them for two additional reasons. One is the conviction that the familiar, indeed entirely traditional and conventional, address to pluralism that Stackhouse's book represents simply has not been intellectually successful. The second reason is the conviction that the root of the failure of the treatment of pluralism represented by Stackhouse lies in its inadequate understanding of "reason."

If there is anything to this speculative account, then the thing that Stackhouse appears to assume need not be argued is the very thing that most needs to be argued — namely, the nature of "reason" and "rationality." It needs to be argued in a noncircular way if the debate is to be significant. That is, critique of another's view in order to support one's own cannot simply assume the validity of one's own view. It may be, furthermore, that explicit and implicit differences about the nature of human reason are at the core of the differences in "anthropology" or views of what it is to be human that we have repeatedly seen to underlie differences about excellence in theological schooling.

Recapitulation

What's theological about theological education? In the current conversation, I suggest, the four proposals we have just examined are good examples of prominent types of approach to this question. At first exposure the relations among them are likely to seem hopelessly confusing. Any two may start at apparently opposite places and then suddenly converge. Others appear to agree about a good bit, but after moving in parallel for a while suddenly diverge, only to intersect with one another again, sometimes with new companions. The pattern of movement among them may appear numbingly complex. However, if we focus on features of each of these proposals that we found instructive and features about which we had reason to be cautious, we will, I think, begin to see the points of tension that give a pattern to their movement.

All parties agree to the point we found instructive in Newman: Education will be unified if it is ordered to a single overarching goal. More particularly, theological education will be unified if all aspects of the enterprise are ordered to "doing theology" in an appropriate way. Furthermore, all parties agree that the chief criterion of this "appropriateness" is that it be done in a way that capacitates students to "do theology" themselves.

But what is "theology"? Here, I think, is the central crux. The question that marks the point of divergence among partners to the conversation is this: What is theology and how is it related to human powers? Put slightly differently: What is it to "do theology" and what do we have to do for people to capacitate them to do it?

One position (that of Stackhouse) holds that Christian theology is largely a kind of theory that can be applied to life. As theory, it claims to be universally valid cross-culturally. It is "objective." Theories engage in human rational powers. The task of exhibiting universally valid truths requires the postulation that human "reason" or "rational power" is universally identical cross-culturally and ahistorically. What kind of theory is theology? The answer to that is determined by the nature and purpose of professional church leadership: it is "church theology." The central purpose of professional church leadership is *apologia* — that is, to formulate and defend theories or "doctrines" about God's truth and God's justice for Christian communities worldwide to apply in their lives in diverse cultural settings. The unity of the "Christian thing" is thus the unity of an internally coherent system of doctrines, a body of theory. Accordingly, what will make education "theological" is that it engages students' rational powers in such a fashion as to capacitate them for rigorous, disciplined, systematic theorizing about God's truth and justice. Theological education is thus a movement from a theory to its application. It will be unified and harmonious education to the extent that it is adequate to the unity of the "Christian thing," exhibiting and advocating the coherence of the whole body of Christian divinity — that is, the theory to be applied. This clearly locates the proposal with the "Berlin" type of excellent education. Theological education is theological because it educates professional church leadership through schooling in historical and, above all, philosophical *Wissenschaft*.

We saw that the picture of our rational powers taken for granted by this position is controversial, and so is its thesis that logically we have to adopt this view of reason to make sense of the enterprise of theological education. That it is controversial among the theological educators who have participated in this debate is no evidence, of course, that Stackhouse's position is wrong or even weak. It may be a "minority" view in this circle, which is not necessarily representative in this regard of theological educators generally; it is very likely to be the "majority" view among professional philosophers, Christian or otherwise (it is, after all, a philosophical issue). However, questions of this sort cannot be settled by majority vote. What is of more immediate concern is the question of the coherence of the proposal. Simply within the framework of Stackhouse's proposal, even if the implied picture of reason is granted, it is unclear that it can coherently hold together the *wissenschaftlich* education required by focus on God's truth and the paideia in piety called for by focus on God's justice.

The other three positions hold that it is precisely the picture of theological education as a movement from theory to application that is at the root of Christian theological education's current inadequacies. They agree that the picture of theology as a body of theory is profoundly misleading, and therefore that theology needs to be reconceived. Furthermore, they agree that theology must be reconceived in such a way that it clearly engages the whole person. Theology must be understood not as something that chiefly engages one's rational powers only but rather as something that engages all one's powers as an integral whole. This is why the "Athens" type of education cannot be abandoned. It is necessary in order to make credible that education in theology effectively bears on the totality of human life in the public realm as well as in the private. The three proposals differ, of course, over how to do this.

Thus a second position holds that Christian theology is a kind of wisdom, perhaps wisdom in being a person in any of the dimensions of human life, private or public (cf. Farley on *theologia*). Here what defines theology is not the nature of professional church leadership (as in the first position), but faith-within-its-situations. Theology is rooted in and grows out of faith-within-its-situations. Theology grows out of a complex whole with both objective and subjective poles: on one side, the objective situation with its many dimensions, including the Christian "mythos," which is comprised of symbols, practices, doctrines, etc.; on the other side, the human subject located in that situation. However, theology is rooted in the subjective pole of this complex. It is faith, one type of subjectivity unreflectively shaped by the total Christian mythos and concretely located in some situation, brought to critically reflective self-awareness. Theology is rooted in and grows out of the whole human subject as shaped by its situation, a situation that includes the Christian mythos. In that sense theology is "subjective." So understood, theology is at once a subject's disposition *(habitus)* to be wise and a subject's capacities to be critically self-reflective in its wisdom (capacities for "dialectical activity"). Despite the many ways in which it is modified in different situations, faith is at bottom one selfsame thing in all faithful people at all times and places. It has the unity, not of a single coherent system of doctrines, but of a single way of being "set" in the world as a person. This is the unity of the "Christian thing." Hence, theology too, both as *habitus* and as a "dialectical activity," is the same in all times and places. Accordingly, what will make schooling "theological" is that it shapes human persons so that they are formed by the *habitus* of theology (paideia) and capacitated to engage in truly critical reflection.

Clearly, this proposal is an instance of the "Athens" type of excellent education modified to incorporate some of the "Berlin" type. Theological education is not a movement *to* anything beyond itself — that is, beyond its forming persons in specific ways. Indeed, it is unified and harmonious precisely to the degree that it stays adequate to the unity of the "Christian thing" by being ordered to the sole end of forming persons in these ways. It modifies the "Athens" model by appropriating the critical inquiry of the "Berlin" model. We saw that it is unclear whether this proposal can coherently incorporate aspects of the "Berlin" type because it is unclear whether the two sides of theology (*habitus* and "dialectical activity") cohere with each other. More seriously, we saw, it is open to the objection that it fails to show how theology bears on the public dimensions of human life; in this view, theology seems confined to the private realm of the interiority of consciousness. The proposal intends to make theology engage the total person. But, the objection goes, the proposal adopts a view of human persons as centers of consciousness above all subjects, a view of faith as a specific mode of that consciousness, and a view of theology as that faith brought to an exquisite level of critical self-awareness. That leaves theology engaged with persons' interiorities; but the proposal leaves it dubious whether or how theology engages persons' public lives.

A third position (that of the Mud Flower Collective) holds that Christian theology is reflection on persons' concrete experiences of relationships, reflection that is ordered to establishing justice. What defines theology here is neither the nature and purpose of professional church leadership nor the nature of faith, but concrete experiences of personal relationships. It is in and with personal relationships that we experience the presence (or absence) of God. As reflection on experiences of personal relationships, theology is something "subjective." It is subjective, but it is not "private," for experiences of personal relationships are always also experiences of the distribution of social, economic, political, and cultural power. Reflection to discern God's presence in personal relationships must also be reflection on the implications of God's presence with regard to the distribution of power — namely, the demand for justice. Hence, theology engages all the powers of a person, both those pertaining to our private lives and those pertinent to our lives in the public realm. At the same time, the concreteness of personal relationships means that theology itself is no one thing. Personal relationships are always located in historical and cultural contexts that differ, often profoundly, from one another. Experiences of God vary as do experiences of relationships. They cannot be reduced to universal common denominators. Hence, as reflection on experiences of personal relationships to discern the presence of God, theology itself will be irreducibly pluralistic.

Accordingly, theological education is a shaping of persons' capacities to hear others' accounts of experiences of personal relationships and of persons' capacities to tell their own stories in such a way as to discern God's presence in those stories. Theological education will be adequate to the irreducible pluralism of modes of experiences of God if it includes within the school itself a pluralism of modes of experience of God that are genuinely "other" by reason of different ethnic, sexual, racial, and social locations. This position evidently belongs with the "Athens" type, but it has been radically modified by the rejection of the assumption that usually goes with paideia — that of a universal "essence" to human nature or to human experience. Indeed, this position rejects the assumption found in the first two positions that there is some universal, ahistorical, cross-cultural "essence" or structure either to theological education's ultimate subject matter or to its course of study. As we saw, it seems necessary that this mode of paideia embrace at least two sorts of *Wissenschaft.* First, it would seem to need to use some body of critical social theory as a tool to help unmask and analyze unjust distributions of power; and second, it would seem to need rigorous and critical reflection, such as is found in the second position, to examine what it means to say that we experience *God* in experiences of personal relationship and indeed how that could be possible. The question then is whether this can be provided without adopting the view of human personhood that seemed troublesome in the second position.

The fourth position (that of Hough and Cobb) holds that Christian theology is critical reflection on the practice of Christian ministry while engaged in Christian ministry. Like the first position, it defines theology by reference to the nature and specific purposes of professional Christian church leadership and not by reference either to faith or to experience of personal relationships in general. But unlike the first position and like the others, it rejects the view that theology is a body of theory to be applied in the practice of ministry. Professional church leadership is defined by reference to the nature and purpose of the church. The church is that community of persons that shares a common distinctively Christian identity. That identity is best described, not by discovering its underlying and universal essence or structure, but by telling the "Christian story" of God's redemptive activity in history, in the public realm. Thus the unity of the "Christian thing" is more like the unity-in-change-and-growth that characterizes the integrity of a living person than like the unity of a systematic body of theory, even a body of theory undergoing correction and emendation.

The church's purpose is to draw attention to what God has been doing for the rest of the world and to respond in gratitude by engaging in those public events in which God may be discerned to be acting redemptively now. Professional church leaders are to be reflective practitioners whose purpose is to assist congregations to keep clear a vision of God redemptively at work today and to test critically how far the church's active response to God's action is consistent with its own identity. To "do theology" is to do these two things in the thick of the church's active engagement in its ministry. Theology engages all the powers of the persons involved in the church's ministry. The criterion by which both vision of God's work and faithfulness of churchly action are tested is the Christian identity the leader shares with the community.

Accordingly, what makes theological education theological in this view is that it is schooling in the results of two sorts of *wissenschaftlich* inquiry: historical research into the "Christian story," which deepens and corrects future leaders' grasp of their Christian identity, and research into the findings of various kinds of studies of the world to sharpen future leaders' capacities for critique of the effectiveness and faithfulness of the church's action in the world. Clearly, this position belongs with the "Berlin" type in its stress on "professional" education, though it has been modified to include paideia-like nurturing of persons' Christian identities. As we saw, however, it seems to be an oddly one-sided version of the "Berlin" type of excellent theological education. While it emphasizes the model's stress on "professional" schooling, it seems, unlike the other three proposals, to deemphasize the model's stress on schooling by way of participation in *Wissenschaft*, in rigorous, methodologically self-conscious inquiry.

We also noted that this position is open to criticism for its unnuanced references to *the* "Christian story," which tend to ignore the demonstrable pluralism of the "Christian thing" and perhaps also by extension the pluralism of "Christian identities." Nonetheless, unlike the second and third positions, this one does not make theology something "subjective." Theology is not faith's critical self-reflectiveness, nor is it personal experience's self-reflectiveness. On the other hand, unlike the first position, it does not make theology out to be something "objective" either. Theology is not the name for a body of universally true doctrine. Nonetheless, it is "objective" in its own way: theology is reflection on the "Christian story" and on communal action in light of that story. Granted, the "story" describes the "identities" of persons and guides the actions of a community of persons. All the same, it is not subjects and subjectivities on which theology reflects, but a single story and public action.

*   *   *

Is it possible to take the best of all four of these positions to form a single picture of theological education? Such a picture of theological schooling would correlate with a picture of the nature of theology; it would pertain to the public as well as the private dimensions of human life; it would be adequate to the pluralism of the "Christian thing" and to the pluralism of the social and cultural worlds in which it is lived; it would be unified without having to assume the sort of universal essence or structure to theological education that belies deep pluralism in the "Christian thing"; and it would retrieve the strengths of both the "Athens" and the "Berlin" types of excellent schooling. In order to do all of these things, such a view would have to find a way to ease the tensions among the voices in the debate to which we have already attended. Perhaps that can be done partly by a fundamental change in the "conceptuality" employed to analyze the basic issues in theological education and to propose resolutions of those issues. In the next chapter we shall examine a proposal that can be read as an effort to do just that by transposing the discussion into a different key.

6

"Athens" and "Berlin" in a New Key?

Is it possible to reconceive what makes theological education theological in such a way that we can honor the agenda of desiderata that has emerged out of our analysis of four major voices in the current debate about theological education? Can we reconceive theological education in such a way that (1) it clearly pertains to the totality of human life, in the public sphere as well as the private, because it bears on all of our powers; (2) it is adequate to genuine pluralism, both of the "Christian thing" and of the worlds in which the "Christian thing" is lived, by avoiding naivete about historical and cultural conditioning without lapsing into relativism; (3) it can be the unifying over-arching goal of theological education without requiring the tacit assumption that there is a universal structure or essence to education in general, or theological inquiry in particular, which inescapably denies genuine pluralism by claiming to be the universal common denominator to which everything may be reduced as variations on a theme; and (4) it can retrieve the strengths of both the "Athens" and the "Berlin" types of excellent schooling, without unintentionally subordinating one to the other?

Charles M. Wood's *Vision and Discernment*

A fifth voice in the conversation suggests that we can. If Farley's modification of the "Athens" model looks like the thesis to which Hough and Cobb's modification of the "Berlin" model is the antithesis, then Charles Wood's proposal may point the way to something like a higher synthesis. In *Vision and Discernment*[1] he proposes a way through this impasse by a radical reorientation of the ways in which we have been posing the central questions. He does this in two important respects: the first is in regard to the standoff between the attempts to show that theology engages the whole person because it is something "subjective" and personal and the attempts to show that it does so because it is something "objective" and public; and the second is in regard to efforts to replace the picture of theology as a movement from theory to practice by new pictures of the relation between theory and practice. We can conveniently review this fifth proposal about what makes theological education theological by explaining the reorientation he suggests on these two points.

The overarching goal of theological education, according to Wood, is theological inquiry. Theological education will be unified when all aspects of it are ordered to that one end. But what is "theology"? After a sketch of the standoff between views of theology as something "objective" and views of it as something "subjective," Wood concurs with Farley's reasons for rejecting the picture of theology as universally valid "objective" truths and factual knowl-

1. Wood, *Vision and Discernment* (Atlanta: Scholars Press, 1985).

edge.[2] He also rejects another type of "objective" view of theology, represented by Hough and Cobb, which defines theology by reference to the purposes of professional church leadership (93).

But Wood then objects to Farley's way of defining theology as a *habitus*. Not that there is anything wrong with the concept of *habitus*. What is wrong is Farley's failure to see the implications of the fact (which he himself notes in passing) that a *habitus* is by definition a disposition for some *activity*. Farley tries to describe theology, which he has already defined as a *habitus*, in terms of the *habitus* for it. But that creates a circle, for no *habitus* can be described except by reference to that for which it is the *habitus* — in this case theology. In Farley's case the circle is broken by introducing a subjective construal of *habitus*, and hence of theology, as a mode of consciousness. But that simply puts us back into the standoff between the views of theology as something "objective" and as something "subjective."

Wood suggests that by following the lead of the concept of *habitus*, but in a different direction from the one Farley took, one can resolve this knot by reconceptualizing the entire issue. We do not have to choose between "objective" and "subjective" construals of what theology is. A *habitus* is a disposition for some activity. Think of theology as an activity, the activity constituted by a type of inquiry, which engages the whole person as an agent, a doer. The *habitus* "is the capacity and disposition to engage in theological inquiry." Thus

> it is the activity of theology — theology as inquiry — *which is theology in the primary sense. It is the "active" sense of the term which is prior;* the "subjective" and "objective" senses are both derivative from it, both logically and chronologically. (34; emphasis added)

2. Wood, p. 32; subsequent citations will be made parenthetically in the text.

Theology in the "objective" sense is chronologically derivative from the activity of theological inquiry because it is the activity that produces objectively valid truth claims and the objective purposes of professional church leadership. Theology in the "subjective" sense is chronologically derivative from the activity of theological inquiry because it is by participation in the activity that one comes to have the appropriate *habitus*, the appropriate mode of subjectivity.

What sort of activity is theology as inquiry? Here Wood introduces his second major proposal to reorient the conversation about what is theological about theological education. Theology, he says, is "critical inquiry into the validity of Christian witness" (21). Theology is one component of the set of activities that comprise the ongoing praxis of Christian communities, for which "witness" is Wood's generic term.

Wood insists on the importance of this point. Against the sort of picture of theological education illustrated by Stackhouse's proposal, Wood rejects the view that theology bears on action as theory applied to *praxis*. He criticizes the "Berlin" type because, while it stresses the importance of theology for the practice of ministry, it fails to stress the way the practice of Christian communities must inform theology (cf. 62-63). For Wood, theological inquiry is part and parcel of the "Christian thing" itself and must not be defined in such a way as to detach it from that practice.

At the same time, however, Wood is dissatisfied with the alternatives offered by the other positions on what's theological about theological schooling. The root of the problem is that, along with their opponents, they all agree to frame the problem and discuss it using the concept pair "theory/practice" (or *theoria/praxis*). In Wood's view, once we agree to do that the problem becomes intractable and the discussion hopelessly, if subtly, muddled. The reason is that the idiom "tends to perpetuate the conventional dichotomy between so-called 'theoretical' (*'wissenschaftlich,'* 'academic') and 'practical' disciplines, and at the same time to promote a false impression of agreement on terms" (63). We systematically undercut ourselves if we try to explain how interrelated theological inquiry and Christian life are by using these categories because they reintroduce the very separation we wish to deny.

Wood proposes that, instead of explaining the relation between theology and action by using the pair "theory/practice," we think about the relation between "vision" and "discernment" in *both* inquiry *and* other types of action. Engaging in *any* action requires both capacities for "insight into particular things or situations in their particularity" (discernment)[3] and capacities for "a general, synoptic understanding of some range of data or field of objects" (vision).[4] Furthermore, the two need each other: "the most complete realization of either comes not at the expense of the other but rather in conjunction with the other's own fuller realization" (75). It is the capacity for critical discernment, not "practice," that serves as a corrective to vision's vulnerability to idolatry and ideological distortion. "*Both* vision and discernment are informed by, and in turn inform, practice. . . . At the same time, vision and discernment *together* — and not vision (or 'theory') alone — are constitutive of theological reflection" (72-73).

The actions that comprise the common life of Christian communities, for which Wood's general name is "witness," require the exercise of capacities for both vision and discernment; theological inquiry, which is but one of the activities that comprise the life of Christian communities, requires them too. Furthermore, all the activities comprising Christian communities are public activities. Theological inquiry is not *applied* to activity, as theory is to practice; it already *is* part of the activity and, like all activity, involves both general synoptic overview and insight into

3. Wood, p. 68.
4. Wood, p. 67.

particulars. In this way Wood honors the concern of the sort of position illustrated by Hough and Cobb to stress theology's public and practical character against the apparent privatizing and interiorizing of it by the position illustrated by Farley. In its own quite different way Wood's proposal also honors the concern of the sort of position illustrated by Stackhouse that Christian theology be kept as fully "public" as is any other way of envisioning and discerning our common world.

With the notion of theology as action that involves both vision and discernment in hand, we may explore what sort of inquiry theology is. "Christian theology may be defined as a critical inquiry into the validity of Christian witness" (21). It is "the self-criticism of the Christian community with regard to its own being and activity as Christian community" (38). Like any inquiry, in Wood's view, it is guided and structured by its *interests*.

The importance of this point to Wood can be shown by contrasting it with Farley's account of theological inquiry. We saw that for Farley theological inquiry is defined as precisely theological by the nature of its subject matter (or "object" of inquiry) — namely, faith-within-its-situations. Furthermore, this subject matter was said to have an essential structure of several dimensions that dictate a structure to theological study. By contrast, for Wood, inquiry is defined as theological, not by the nature of its subject matter ("Christian witness"), but by its interests *in* its subject matter. We are free to be interested in the literary qualities of Christian witness, or in its history, or in its role in social control, but inquiry guided by such interests would be literary criticism, or history, or social analysis, not theology. What would make it theology is an interest in its being true to itself as, precisely, Christian witness. What makes an inquiry into Christian witness Christian theology is that it is guided by an interest to judge that witness "by the standards which pertain to it precisely as Christian witness. . . . this is what was meant by calling it a critical inquiry into the *validity* of Christian witness" (26). This is the activity that is theological inquiry.

Critical inquiry into the validity of Christian witness is not a simple activity. Its guiding interest has three dimensions, each of which can be expressed in a question. The questions elicit a double response. On one side, they invite critical judgment of an instance of Christian witness: Is it valid? On the other side, they invite constructive proposals: In these circumstances, what would be a valid witness? (Cf. 40.) The three leading questions are these:

(1) Is this piece of verbal or nonverbal witness genuinely Christian? As Christian witness, it claims truly to represent Jesus Christ. Does it? (Cf. 39.) Wood calls critical inquiry guided by this question "historical theology." He defines historical theology as

> the use of the resources and methods of historical study to pursue the theological question of the "Christianness," i.e., the faithfulness to what is normatively Christian, of Christian witness. (42)

Wood includes critical inquiry into the Bible here, for what is at stake in historical theology is identification of the criteria by which to test the faithfulness of witness to Jesus Christ.

(2) Is this piece of witness true? (Cf. 39.) Wood calls critical inquiry guided by this question "philosophical theology."

> The philosophical study of any human activity aims at exhibiting the "logic" of that activity, that is, at uncovering the principles relevant to its understanding and criticism.

So the adjective "philosophical" here indicates "the methodological orientation of this branch of theological inquiry" (45). Philosophical theology goes "beyond the identification of criteria and procedures for judgment to the making of actual judgments concerning the meaning and truth of Christian witness" (46).

(3) Is this piece of verbal or nonverbal witness "fittingly enacted? Is it appropriately related to its context?" (40). Wood calls critical inquiry guided by this question "practical theology." Practical theology

> draws upon the resources of those disciplines concerned with the understanding of human culture and behavior — psychology, sociology, anthropology, history, and their various offspring — to inquire about the relationship between the content and intention of Christian witness and its context. (48)

It is not narrowly concerned with the practice of church leadership "but rather with the enactment of Christian witness in its entirety — that is, with the entire life and activity of the church as the community of witness" (48).

These three dimensions of critical theological inquiry are distinguishable from one another, but they are inseparably interdependent. They are distinguishable because they are guided by different aims. We can pursue any one of them without having any interest in either of the other two (cf. 50). Furthermore, each of them is made rigorously critical by incorporating the relevant "secular" disciplines of history, philosophy, or the human sciences. Theological inquiry is not simply dependent upon these other inquiries and their results: "It does not just involve individual questions which also happen to have a home in other inquiries." Rather, "one pursues a certain part of the theological task *by* engaging in historical inquiry, and another part *by* philosophical inquiry, and so on" (37; cf. 58). When one actively participates in sociological inquiry toward answering the leading question "Is this piece of witness fittingly enacted?" one is not engaging in nontheological inquiry. Nor is one engaging in nontheological inquiry when one actively participates in historical inquiry toward answering the question "Is this Christian witness faithful?" — nor when actively engaged in philosophical inquiry toward answering the leading question "Is this witness true?" In each case, what makes the inquiry theological is the leading question, which in each case is one dimension of theological inquiry as such. Theology subsumes under its guiding interest the aims guiding each of these other inquiries. However, the methods proper to each of these types of inquiry discipline the relevant dimension of theological inquiry, making it rigorously critical, but also making it distinguishable from the other two.

For all their distinguishability, these three are nonetheless inseparably interdependent dimensions of a single inquiry. Even if one pursued "any one of these inquiries without an *interest* in the other two, one may not pursue any of them without becoming involved in at least some aspects of the other two" (50). Because theology is critical inquiry into the validity of Christian witness in *every* respect (faithfulness to itself, truth, fittingness), historical, philosophical, and practical theology are necessarily "in reciprocal relationship to each other" (67). They are not three steps or stages in a sequence.

The relations among them cannot be clarified by using the contrast "theory/practice." It simply muddles things to agree to debate whether the movement is from the constructive and critical theory delivered by historical and philosophical theology to the practice analyzed by practical theology, or whether the movement is from the praxis examined by practical theology (even as "practical thinking") to historical and philosophical theology taken as reflection "on" practice or taken as theory derived "from" practice (cf. the sort of position on theological education illustrated by Hough and Cobb). Nor is there any intrinsic dialectical movement or structure to theological inquiry that could be brought out by clarifying the relation between "theory" and "practice" in the abstract, or the relation between prereflective and reflective knowing, or the relation between foundational knowledge and interpretive skills (cf. the sort of position on theological education illustrated by Farley). Any two dimensions of theological inquiry are necessary to and inform the third. In particular, judgments about the faithfulness (historical theology) or the truth (philosophical theology) of Christian witness must presuppose and take into account (and not simply lead into) analysis of the context of that witness and its fittingness to that context (cf. 50).

Furthermore, each of the three dimensions of theological inquiry is in certain respects both "practical" and "theoretical." Each involves the acquisition and employment (or practice) of certain abilities, and each involves reflection on the practice of witness, normally with the practical aim of making better practice. Each of them — practical theology included — is also theoretical: each requires for its effective pursuit the exercise of *theoria* — that is, the comprehensive envisioning of both the Christian witness and the theological task in their unity and complexity (cf. 67). Because the contrast "theory/practice" is in some sense present in all three of these dimensions, it cannot help to explain the relation of inseparable interdependence among the three dimensions of theological inquiry.

What does help to illumine the reciprocal interdependence of the three dimensions of theological inquiry, Wood proposes, is the distinction "vision/discernment." Theological inquiry involves "a dialectical relationship between vision and discernment" (69) in each of its three dimensions. In each dimension it is necessary to envision "Christian witness as a whole" (i.e., the "Christian thing" as some sort of unity). In each dimension we "will draw upon whatever resources seem most promising for discovering and explicating its content [i.e., the content of Christian witness] so as to provide an answer to the complex question of its validity" (69). In philosophical theology those resources will be philosophers' resources; in historical theology they will be historians' resources. Wood especially stresses the importance of resources from the social sciences that practical theology brings into play in envisioning Christian witness as a whole:

> They can contribute to an understanding of oneself, one's social context, one's loyalties, etc., which can enable one to detect the presence and influence of the hidden factors shaping one's theological thinking and one's presentation of the Christian witness. (71)

Because the three dimensions of theological inquiry are reciprocally interdependent, the three types of envisioning Christian witness as a whole are also interdependent. For an adequate vision of Christian witness as a whole we need the interplay between visions of that witness that draw on all three types of resources — historical, philosophical, and social scientific.

In each dimension discernment is also necessary:

> The activity of discernment in theology is the effort to grasp and assess the character of a particular instance of Christian witness — past, present, or prospective. It is the effort to see what is really there in the situation, rather than merely what one has been led to expect.

There is a discernment "proper to each dimension of theological inquiry" (73). Historical discernment,

> rather than viewing each individual character or incident as only an instance of some collectivity or trend, is able to see the specific, the novel . . . the way even the "typical" diverges from type . . . [and can] recognize the peculiar dialectic between continuity and discontinuity in tradition. (73)

Philosophical discernment, which "involves a keen logical and conceptual discrimination, . . . fight[s] the 'craving for generality' (73-74). (Cf. the Mud Flower Collective's critique of misplaced universalizing!) Practical discernment involves "a sensitivity to the human situation, and the conceptual equipment to appraise particular actions in context" (74). (Is it deliberate or inadvertent activity? What are its motives, its consequences? etc.) Because the three dimensions of theological inquiry are reciprocally interdependent, the three types of discernment of instances of Christian witness are also interdependent. For adequate discernment of any instance of witness, we need the interplay of historical, philosophical, and social scientific discernment.

The full set of modes of "visioning" Christian witness as a whole and the full set of modes of discernment of instances of Christian witness must be kept dialectically related to one another in the interest of keeping critical theological inquiry *self*-critical. All three modes of theological discernment are necessary as a *corrective* to theological vision's tendency to distort ideologically, to ascribe universal validity to the limited and particular, and to gloss over ambiguity and tragedy in experience. The self-critical character of theological inquiry cannot be explained by using the "theory/practice" contrast, for "it is discernment, and not 'practice,' which is the proper counterpoint to theory or vision in this respect. . . . *Both* vision and discernment are informed by, and in turn inform, practice" (72).

The singularity or unity of theological inquiry in and through its three dimensions is the ground, in Wood's view, for two more theological "disciplines," in addition to philosophical theology, historical theology, and practical theology. When one's aim is "to integrate these three basic inquiries in a comprehensive and constructive fashion" (50), one is doing *systematic theology*. The defining interest in systematic theology is the *unity* of the three dimensions of critical inquiry into the validity of Christian witness. Systematic theology aims to formulate not only critical but constructive proposals that comprehensively integrate both the ways in which probes of the fruitfulness, truth, and fittingness of the witness *envision* the "Christian thing" as a whole and the ways in which these probes *discern* particular instances of the "Christian thing." So far as the "visioning" aspect of theological inquiry is concerned,

> this means, e.g., asking how social-scientific accounts of human behavior (say, in cultural anthropology) might illuminate historical inquiry, and how both might bear on philosophical questions regarding meaning and truth, in regard to Christian tradition. (71)

And so far as the discerning aspect is concerned, this means

> what we might call "systematic discernment" . . . a multidimensional insight into the particular character of a situation, in which one is attentive to the interplay of various sorts of factors. (73)

The other additional theological discipline is *moral theology.* Like systematic theology, moral theology's basis is the unity of the three dimensions of theological inquiry. Its defining interest is the "validity of Christian witness concerning human conduct" (54), personal and communal, individual and institutional. Where practical theology is concerned with assessing the conduct of Christian witness as witness, moral theology is concerned with assessing Christian witness as conduct (cf. 55).

Because both systematic and moral theology are defined by interests in the integral unity of the "Christian thing" and the unity of theological inquiry, neither of them should be thought of as the "middle discipline" (cf. 50-51) between historical theology's formulations of what is normatively or faithfully "Christian" and practical theology's application of those formulations to practice. Schleiermacher had arranged them in precisely that fashion, and ever since then, that picture of the essential movement of theological schooling has ruled wherever the "Berlin" model of excellence in theological education has been adopted. That created a one-way movement in theological inquiry in which practical theology depends on systematic and moral theology, but they do not depend on it.

And *that,* Wood holds, is what creates the central problem for theology, which people try to formulate and then solve using the "theory/practice" distinction. It is better to say that systematic theology and moral theology are not brokers between "theory" and "practice"; rather, both systematic theology and moral theology are inquiry defined by an interest in the unity of the three reciprocally interrelated dimensions of theological inquiry. Construed in that way, systematic and moral theology are "informed, methodologically and materially, by practical theological reflection as well as by the other two basic inquiries" (51).

If we were to adopt Wood's way of understanding what theology is, what picture of theological schooling would follow? Wood points out that there are two uses of theological inquiry, the "normal" use and the "educational" use. The normal use of theological inquiry "is the attainment of considered judgements concerning Christian witness." These may be judgments critical of some instance of Christian witness, or they may be constructive judgments proposing what Christian witness properly is. Making such judgments requires certain capacities, especially capacities for vision and for discernment. "The educational use of theological inquiry also involves the making of judgments," but in contrast to normal use

> its more proper aim is not the formation of judgments, but the formation of judgment. . . . It informs practice by equipping the practitioner not with ready-made deliberative judgments but rather with the capacity to make them. (80)

Wood goes on to say that

it is not the mere possession of "a theology" that is the measure of a theological education; it is rather one's ability to form, revise, and employ theological judgments that counts. Vision and discernment are exhibited in practice. (82)

Hence the overarching goal that will unify theological schooling is the goal of helping people to acquire "that complex set of intellectual and personal qualities which go to make up what we might still call the theological *habitus*" (79) — that is, to make sound theological judgments.

How is such judgment formed? By engaging people in the activity of theological inquiry. Accordingly, Wood's proposal no more implies any particular radical form of the abstract structure of the received fourfold curriculum than has any of the other proposals we have examined. What is required, rather, is an expansion of our view of the place of theology in the total curriculum, structured pretty much as it now is.

This does not mean an increase in the number of courses required in systematic theology. It has rather to do with the *questions* that guide teaching and learning in every course. It means "understanding the entire curriculum as really and truly a theological curriculum, that is, as a body of resources ordered to the cultivation in students of an aptitude for theological inquiry" (94). The leading question in every course dealing with any subject matter must be this: How does this subject matter (be it "logic, or Mexican-American history, or the sociology of religion") contribute to assessing the validity of Christian witness? When this question expresses the dominant interest governing the inquiry, then it can subsume the interests that define the several academic disciplines. The student is helped to acquire the aptitudes needed in order to do history or philosophy or a social science *as* aptitudes needed to inquire critically into the validity of Christian witness.

Wood is not much troubled by the fact, which so disturbs Farley and Hough and Cobb, that the way in which academic disciplines are institutionalized in American higher education also dictates the structure of the curricula of theological schools. The five theological disciplines that Wood identifies, which in their reciprocal interplay comprise theological inquiry, do not, he cheerfully acknowledges, correspond to the academic disciplines and "disciplinary specialties" (to use Farley's terms) that organize theological schools' curricula into departments of "Old Testament," "New Testament," "Church History," "American Religious History," and so forth. Indeed, in his view,

> theological inquiry . . . does not depend absolutely upon the existence of a corresponding disciplinary arrangement. It can be conducted, with more or less success, within a great variety of arrangements, each of which may facilitate the inquiry in some respects, and obstruct or distort it in others. A certain tension is likely to exist between any lively inquiry and the disciplinary traditions. (57)

Not that the five theological disciplines can do without the established academic disciplines. As we saw, for Wood, one actively engages in the discipline of philosophy or history or a social science *in* doing theology. The guiding interest of theological inquiry simply subsumes the interests guiding academic disciplines. In regard to the institutionalization of the disciplines, the five theological disciplines are now only "potential disciplines." Perhaps the pressure of the guiding interest of theological inquiry will so shape theological engagement in history, philosophy, social sciences, etc., as to make the theological disciplines actual — that is, institutionalized in their own right. If so, Wood believes, "it will only be by a gradual, deliberate process of transformation" (59). In the meantime, Wood appears to be sanguine that if the leading question of theological inquiry is kept explicitly in view, it is powerful enough not only to subsume the leading interest of each of the relevant academic disciplines but also to resist distortions that the institutionalization of the academic disciplines might tend to impose on theology.

Does this picture of theological schooling belong with the "Athens" or the "Berlin" type of excellent education? Perhaps it modifies both of them so much more than any of the other four types that it amounts to a third way. In this respect Wood's proposal is particularly instructive. In accord with one pole of the "Berlin" type, Wood stresses that what makes theological schooling excellent schooling is that it is schooling in the capacities for rigorous disciplined *Wissenschaft*. Wood endorses the view that when we are engaged in the "educational use" of theology the stress must fall on "*how* to think rather than *what* to think," even though that "may look like evasion" (81) of the validity of Christian witness. In accord with the "Athens" type, Wood insists that what makes theological schooling excellent schooling is that it shapes sound theological judgment; through this paideia we acquire a *habitus,* albeit a *habitus* for action that is self-critical in the modern sense of "critique" — a sense that ancient Athens knew nothing of.

What sets Wood's proposal apart is the way in which he explicates the capacities both for *Wissenschaft* and for the *habitus.* They turn out to be the same kind of thing. In both cases acquiring them is a matter of acquiring certain *conceptual* capacities; but "concept" is understood here in a special way — the concepts that must be acquired are abilities or aptitudes. Acquiring some concepts is a "self-involving" matter, "in that a grasp of them requires (or, perhaps better: amounts to) a certain capacity to understand *oneself* by them" (86). Many theological concepts are like that — "creation," "sin," "grace," and "hope," for example. Acquiring these concepts shapes one's identity in a significant way. Moreover, learning some of these concepts involves learning to understand oneself critically. To be rigorously critical in inquiry "is more like a 'character-trait' than like a skill" (88).

Accordingly, what is needed for *wissenschaftlich* theological inquiry — that is, inquiry to understand and probe the validity of Christian witness — is not best understood as a methodological and hermeneutical self-consciousness (in opposition both to Farley, who understands what is needed for *wissenschaftlich* inquiry in just that way and celebrates it, and Hough and Cobb who understand it that way and minimize its importance). Rather, what is needed is the acquisition of certain capacities and aptitudes, the mastery of which shapes who one is. This makes it sound, ironically, as though the way to acquire *wissenschaftlich* disciplines is through some kind of paideia (which is precisely Farley's claim). Not only does Wood distance himself from the "Berlin" model's picture of what is involved in education in *Wissenschaft*, he also rejects its definition of theological education as professional schooling: "Theological education is not necessarily professional education for ministry, but the heart of proper professional education for ministry *is* theological education" (93). (Here Wood sides with Farley and against Hough and Cobb.)

So too, what is involved in acquiring the theological *habitus* is mastering certain concepts — that is, acquiring abilities and aptitudes for making sound judgments. Here too, having the relevant concepts is "more like a 'character-trait' than like a skill." However, this is not understood in the way in which the "Athens" type understands paideia. For Wood we do not need to posit something ahistorically and cross-culturally universal to all human beings, something "objective" like an invisible and immortal soul (which paideia presupposed in ancient Athens), of which "dispositions" and "character traits" are modifications. Nor need we think of "dispositions" and "character traits" as modifications of something "subjective" like the universal structures of human consciousness (which paideia and *habitus* presuppose for Farley).

In Wood's view it is enough to understand acquisition of *habitus* as something that we *do*, whatever our "nature" may be.

Perhaps the major difference between Wood and the other proposals we have examined (except for the Mud Flower Collective's proposal) is located here, at the point of explicitly or implicitly assumed anthropology or view of what a human being is. Wood neither assumes nor implies any claims about an "essence" that is universal to all human beings in every time and place and that is constitutive of our humanity. Universal claims are made or implied that all human beings act in a variety of ways and that all human beings can acquire some of the capacities needed for engaging in some kinds of action. Unless "shaping" is all that is required for education to count as paideia, which is much too broad and vague to serve as a definition, it is difficult to see how Wood's picture of theological schooling belongs any more to the "Athens" type of excellent education than to the "Berlin" model.

What makes Wood's proposal distinctive in this regard and may be its greatest strength is his suggestion that "theology" be understood in an "active sense" rather than as something "objective" or as something "subjective." However, the suggestion is also the point at which his development of his proposal is worrisome.

The proposal has the advantage of not bringing with it any assumptions about a universal, cross-cultural, ahistorical structure to theological education. That is an advantage because it makes it possible to frame a proposal about what is theological about theological education that can consistently address both the issue of the schooling's adequacy to the ideal unity of the "Christian thing" and its adequacy to several types of pluralism. The schooling will be unified when the overarching goal of all of its activities is the cultivation of persons' capacities for theological judgment in their conduct of theological inquiry. At the same time, this proposal is consistent with acknowledging several kinds of pluralism. To acknowledge pluralism is to acknowledge the presence, not simply of diversity, but of a diversity that is not subtly or overtly reduced to a set of variations on an underlying theme. It is to acknowledge the presence of types of "otherness" without assuming that they all share in some one set of common denominators. The proposal is consistent, first, with acknowledging a pluralism of ways in which the "Christian thing" has been and is now construed. The unity of theological schooling need not rest on an implicit or tacit privileging of one construal over others. The way in which the goal of theological schooling is formulated is also consistent with acknowledging a genuine pluralism in the social worlds to which graduates of the school may go and in which the "Christian thing" is lived out. In each of these cases Wood's proposal is consistent with acknowledgment of pluralism because the proposal assumes no universal structure in "human nature" — neither a universal structure of "reason" nor one of "consciousness" — to which these pluralisms could be reduced as to a least common denominator.

Wood is clear and explicit about ways in which social and cultural factors ideologically distort both Christian witness and theological inquiry. However, it is worrisome that his analysis of the activity of theological inquiry and of the activity of schooling *in* that inquiry devotes so little attention to the institutionalization of either. It focuses little attention on institutional arrangements of power within a theological school, or on the consequences of the activity of theological inquiry on a theological school's own social, economic, and cultural location.

Attention to these matters would seem to be required, however, by the proposal itself. Human activity is always shaped by cultural patterns and social structures. Insistence on the importance of that point for theological education is one of the major contributions of the Mud Flower Collective to the agenda of the debate about what makes theological education theological. A failure to explore how the activity of theological inquiry is located in and inescapably shaped by patterns of activity that are dictated by its social and cultural setting and, just as important, patterns that are dictated by institutional power arrangements, deprives theological inquiry of the means for its self-criticism and correction. One point at which this issue is broached in Wood's proposal, as we saw, has to do with the effect on theological schooling of the institutionalization of the academic disciplines in which theological inquiry participates (including philosophical, historical, and social scientific inquiries). As we noted, Wood seemed to be remarkably optimistic about the abilities of theological inquiry to resist corruption from this quarter.

It is troubling that this issue is not explored with the same intent that Farley, for example, had in building into theological schooling moments for self-examination and self-correction against corruption from such sources. At the same time, however, it may well be that Wood's proposal to understand theology as an *activity* provides the most promising conceptual resources for doing just that. Not only are intentional human actions in large part given their specific shape and significance by their cultural "location," but they are also guided by human interests that themselves have specific social, economic, and cultural locations. These aspects of human action are part of what makes them what they concretely are in every particular case. Thus this "locatedness" of intentional action is the basis for the fact that actions can be both authentic and ideologically distorted.

The point is that remarks about the potentially distorting and demonic effects of actions' locatedness do not need to be added extrinsically, as it were, to analyses of human inquiry — here theological inquiry in particular — cast in terms of "action"; such remarks are entailed *in* the very concept of action. The concept of action *itself* brings with it the requirement that a full characterization of any action must include, precisely in order to be "full," attention to the ways in which the action is socially located and may be distorted ideologically and otherwise. Thus a characterization of theology and of what makes theological education theological that is cast, like Wood's, in terms of "action" already has conceptually built into it resources for addressing the justice issues so central to the sort of position illustrated by the Mud Flower Collective's proposal.

*   *   *

Throughout our review of Wood's proposal about what makes theological education theological we have been noting points of convergence with and divergence from the other four voices in this conversation. This has served to underscore the centrality of the agenda that has been growing as this review has proceeded. At the same time we have consistently seen that the "conceptuality" that Wood has adopted undercuts fundamental matters on which the other four voices tacitly agreed, with the effect that in his proposal the issues appear to be addressed in a different key, in which many of the tensions noted among the other four conversation partners were significantly eased. Thus Wood's proposal adds an important new issue to the agenda: In what conceptuality do we most *fruitfully* formulate the basic issues confronting theological education today, propose resolutions of those issues, and debate our disagreements? We will now turn in the conclusion of this book to a summary of the issues, and the morals about how best to discuss the issues, that has emerged from this review of the recent literature on what is theological about theological education.

Epilogue: Morals of the Tale

W hat makes theological education theological? Four major
families of issues have emerged in the course of our review of
the major books contributing to the recent discussion of this question. Two of the issues are explicitly clear to the writers. One of these
is a set of issues generated by theological education's need to address
pluralism. The other is a set of issues generated by theological
education's need for unity. Two more issues turn out to be implicit in
what contributors to this discussion wrote. One of these is generated
by theological education's need to negotiate between two ultimately
unsynthesizable types of excellent education, "Athens" and "Berlin."
The last is an issue about how best to formulate conceptually both
the issues and the proposed resolutions of the issues.

Issues of Pluralism and of Unity

Our review of literature on the nature and purpose of theological
education suggested several points about how to address issues of

pluralism and unity. The central positive moral about how best to address both issues of unity and issues of pluralism has repeatedly been this: Focus on the *end* of theological education, not on its methods or structure; conceptualize theological education teleologically and not functionally or formally. Some efforts to deal with issues raised by pluralism and by fragmentation focus on pedagogical methods and on the functions comprising the educational process. There can be no question about the enormous importance of these matters. Theological education would benefit immeasurably from a great deal more sophistication in these regards. However, attention to these functional matters will not deal with the roots of the issues raised by pluralism and fragmentation because they do not identify and clarify the overarching end of the entire enterprise of theological education. Improved pedagogy and revised educational processes may make existing schooling function better educationally, but they will not of themselves make it more adequate to the facts of pluralism or to the need for unity.

More often, efforts to deal with fragmentation and pluralism focus on reforming the curriculum of a school. Issues raised by several sorts of pluralism are addressed by adding some courses and rearranging some existing courses into new "programs." Issues raised by fragmentation are dealt with by organizing the formal structure of the school's array of already defined courses. Curricular reorganization is certainly not irrelevant. However, attention to these formal matters will not deal with the roots of the issues raised by pluralism and fragmentation because it does not challenge the ways in which the component courses are themselves defined and designed; it simply rearranges them. The more basic issues have to do with the relation between the overarching end of theological education and the respective ends of individual courses. Resolution of the basic issues turns on just how the end of theological education is understood.

Our literature review yielded at least four morals about how *not* to address issues raised by pluralism and by fragmentation in theological schooling. The first of these "negative" morals is this: Focus on clarifying the end of theological education, but do not define that end as the training of clergy; in other words, avoid what Edward Farley calls the "clergy paradigm" of theological schooling. The point here is not to denigrate the importance of educating clergy; nor is it to deny that education of clergy is embraced by theological education. Rather, it is to urge that the end to which theological education is ordered, whatever it may be, is an end that is basic to the well-being of far more walks of life than just the peculiar calling of the clergy. Further, experience has shown that theological education *defined* as clergy education suffers from the "happiness paradox": that is, just as we cannot achieve happiness by a course of life defined by the pursuit of happiness, so we cannot achieve the education of superlative church leaders by a course of study defined by the roles and tasks of church leadership.

Closely related to the warning against the clergy paradigm, a second negative moral pointed out by our literature review is this: Focus on clarifying the end of theological education, but avoid definitions of that end that are explicitly or implicitly individualistic. Of course, it is individual students who learn, and in the end each individual student has to do his or her own learning. Moreover, people learn in different ways; there is no doubt about the desirability of designing schooling to be as individualized as possible. What is at stake here, however, is not the pedagogy but the view of human personhood that is implied by schooling. Inherent in Christian understandings of the realities of the human condition and of what personhood might be if it were set free to flourish, and in Christian understandings of society and church, is a strong stress on human sociality and an equally strong resistance to the ways in which individualistic views of personhood erode or deny sociality. A theological account of what is theological about a theological school ought not to become complicit with individualistic pictures of what it is to be a learner and a teacher.

A third negative moral arising from our literature review is this: Focus on clarifying the end of theological education, but do not define that end by reference to *the* "essence" or "underlying structure" or "identity" of faith or of the "Christian thing" or of "*the* church." For one thing, to do so begs far too many issues raised by different sorts of pluralism. While there surely are important family resemblances among various actual communities who call themselves Christian churches, it is far from clear that they all share some one thing called "the essence of the church." No doubt there are family resemblances among different concrete practices and symbols of the Christian life, but it is far from clear that they are all expressions and manifestations of some *one* underlying "structure" or "essence" of faith-as-such. No doubt there are family resemblances among differing construals of the "Christian thing," but it is far from clear that they are all variations on the "essence" of Christianity or of Christian theology. It is unlikely that the basic issues raised in theological schooling by the pluralism of pluralisms that confronts it will be addressed at their root if the end of theological schooling is defined in so essentialist or formalist a way.

This way of defining the end of theological schooling, furthermore, risks dealing with issues raised by fragmentation in distorted ways. As we saw in our examination of Newman's rationale for including theology in the curriculum of a university and in other proposals to overcome fragmentation in theological schooling, it is very difficult to give material content to the idea of an "essence" that unifies schooling without its becoming dangerously open to ideological distortion. The danger of proceeding in this way is that one may unify theological schooling but in doing so may hide larger inequities in the arrangement of social power and may validate particular oppressive arrangements of power.

A fourth negative moral is this: Focus on clarifying the end of theological schooling, but avoid doing so in a way that systematically disengages theology and lives of faith, both communal and individual, from the public realm. This appears to be what happens, however unintentionally, when issues raised by pluralism and by fragmentation are dealt with by construing theological schooling as a movement from "source of wisdom" to "wise living," or from "basis-of-theory" to "application-of-theory," or from a mode of "inwardness" or "subjectivity" to "outward manifestation and expression." The tendency to talk in this way is understandable. The combination of issues raised by fragmentation and by pluralism looks easier to deal with if the issues raised by fragmentation can be confined to the "ivory tower" realm of academic theory and only subsequently applied to the pluralistic, public "real world"; it looks easier to deal with if issues raised by pluralism can be confined to the private realm of consciousness and only subsequently expressed in the public realm. However, the former misconstrues the relation between theology and action, as though theology were theory systematized in the academy to be applied in practical cases later on; and the latter misconstrues the relevant pluralisms, as though they were alternative outward and public manifestations of a single mode of inwardness. In each of these cases theology and the life of faith are systematically disengaged from the public realm, and then have to be reconnected to it by a move that turns out to be very difficult or even impossible to make.

Issues Involved with Negotiating
between "Athens" and "Berlin"

Our literature review also suggested several points about the third set of issues, which has to do with negotiating between the "Athens" and "Berlin" types of excellent education. These issues were implicit in the literature; we had to tease them out of the discussion in the course of our review. The central "positive" moral about how best to negotiate between these two models is this: Focus on the nature of the basic *movement* of theological study as a theological question, not as a question about the psychology of learning, nor even as a question about the logical relations among various subjects studied in theological education. The question to be asked, then, is this: Is it most theologically adequate to see the movement of theological education as a movement from source (of "revelation," of "wisdom about God," etc.) to personal appropriation; or as a movement from source to application of source in life (especially, perhaps, the life of church leadership); or as a movement from source, to doctrines implicit in the source, to applications of doctrines to life's problems; or as a movement from sources, to theories about the sources, to applications of those theories to life; or in some other way? Every answer to the question about the theological adequacy of any particular picture of the movement of theological education is tied to some picture of the nature of Christian theology itself. As we saw, different understandings of the nature of theology bring with them different implications about the movement of specifically theological education, and vice versa. Too often the answer to this question is left implicit in proposals about the nature and purpose of theological education, and the answer's coherence with the view of theology that the proposals adopt is left unexamined.

This positive moral brings with it several negative ones. If you judge that theological education is some version of a movement from source to personal appropriation, you will negotiate from within the "Athens" type of excellent education and on its terms. Very well. However, do not suppose that it is adequate to negotiate with "Berlin" simply by appropriating the stress of the "Berlin" type on theological education as "professional" education (construed as paideia-like "clergy formation") while minimizing its stress on *Wissenschaft*. Theologically speaking, "Athens" as a type of excellent education is insufficiently capable of critique of its own idolatries and susceptibilities to ideological distortions. It needs the "Berlin" model's stress on *wissenschaftlich* inquiry to radicalize its own traditional form of "critical" thinking in the direction of ideology critique. On the other hand, if you appropriate the "Berlin" model's stress on *Wissenschaft* on the "Athens" model's terms (*wissenschaftlich* education as paideia-like "formation" in capacities for critical inquiry) do not suppose that you can omit the other pole of "professional" education, for as we have seen, *Wissenschaft* is theologically relevant only insofar as it is tied to *church* leadership roles. The "Athens" type's theological insufficiency in the face of our tendencies toward cognitive idolatry and ideological self-serving means that it needs the *Wissenschaft* pole of the "Berlin" type as a corrective; but it cannot appropriate that without distorting what it appropriates unless it also appropriates the "professional" education pole, and vice versa.

Conversely, if you judge that theological education is some version of the movement from source to application, then you will negotiate from within the "Berlin" model of excellent education and on its terms. Very well. However, do not suppose that it is theologically sufficient to appropriate "Athens" solely into the "professional" education pole of theological education on the "Berlin" model's terms (construing "professional" education as, say, paideia into the *habitus* of faith). As we saw, "professional"

227

education according to the "Berlin" type is, theologically speaking, too open to individualistic and functionalist corruptions and in need of the inherently social and collegial character of the "Athens" type's paideia. However, if the goal of one pole of theological education is cultivation of capacities for *Wissenschaft*, and if the goal of the other pole is cultivation of faith's *habitus*, theological education ends up with two overarching goals and is inherently incoherent. In any case, the "Berlin" model's *Wissenschaft* pole is also too individualistic, theologically speaking, and in need of correction by the "Athens" type's paideia. If "Athens" is to be appropriated into "Berlin" on the "Berlin" model's terms, it must be incorporated into both of its poles.

In either case, never suppose that you can synthesize the two types of excellent theological education. It may be that for historical reasons no American theological education can abandon either type. All the same, the tensions between them are unavoidable. The best that can be hoped for is an unstable truce, constantly threatening to break down into educational incoherence. The underlying reason for this is that each type presupposes a different view of the nature of "reason" and, indeed, a different view of "human nature." A decision to negotiate from within one of these two types and on its grounds is at the same time, however implicitly, a decision to adopt its underlying assumptions about what it is to be human. One's "appropriation" of aspects of the other type, then, is always a matter of abstracting it from its conceptual home in one kind of view of "reason" and "human nature" and grafting it into an alien conceptual field. As a result, the seeds of conceptual confusion about the nature and purpose of theological education, if not seeds of outright incoherence, are as omnipresent as they appear to be historically unavoidable.

Issues of Conceptual Formulation of the Discussion

Finally, our literature review yielded important morals about *formal* features of discussions about what makes theological education theological. The decisive moral in this regard seems to be this: Examine with great care the conceptuality that is taken for granted by all parties to a debate — especially if the debate shows signs of becoming interminable. It is very likely that the fruitlessness of the debate is rooted in the *way* or the *conceptuality* in which the issues have been posed. In particular, examine closely the contrast terms everybody seems to have agreed to use. For example, are there ways in which such conventional contrasts as "theory/practice" or "academic/professional" or "objective/subjective" serve as much to obfuscate issues as to clarify them? How far do the pictures of the nature of theology that underwrite proposals about the nature and purpose of theological education require misleading distinctions? How far do assumed pictures of the nature of "reason" and "human being" dictate the proposals? More ambitiously, is there some alternative conceptuality, hopefully one that is modest and unelaborate, that would clarify where conventional terms obscure, and that would allow us to pose fresh and productive questions where conventional questions have proven unfruitful? This moral is an invitation to think as hard about the formal features of the debate as we think about its material content when we are caught up in it.

Index

Academic freedom, 15, 52, 69
Advancement of Theological Education, The (by Niebuhr, Williams, and Gustafson), 64-71, 79-81, 83-84, 87, 90
Apologetics, 183-84
Aristotle, 45
Association of Theological Schools (formerly American Association of Theological Schools, AATS), 56, 64, 67
"Athens" model of schooling, 6-11, 48. *See also* Paideia
"Berlin" modifications of, 192
human nature in, 26, 44-47, 122
internal movement of, 19-20
Newman's modifications of, 30-47
and teaching, 20
Wissenschaft and, 227

"Berlin" model of schooling, 12-19, 24, 25, 90-91. *See also Wissenschaft;* Professional education
in America, 49-51, 54-64
bipolar character of, 18, 23, 77-78, 157-58
human nature in, 26-27
internal movement of, 22
as needing "Athens" corrective, 227-28
public character of, 25
and teaching, 23, 68-69
Brown, William Adams, 54-65, 72, 81

Cannon, Katie G., 135
"Christian thing." *See also* "Essences," universal: of Christianity
construals of, 97-98, 103, 149, 190, 192, 195
pluralism of, 98-99, 134
truth claims and, 176-77
Church, 16, 53
Hough and Cobb on, 159-63
Niebuhr on, 72-74
and theological school, 77, 81, 171
and worship, 162-63

231

Church leadership. *See also* Professional education
 ideological distortion of, 82-83, 158
 as "management," 163-66
 "pastoral director" model of, 72, 74-76, 82
 and theological education, 16, 24, 116
Clement of Alexandria, 11
Clement of Rome, 10-11
Clergy, social status of, 53, 57, 62
Cobb, John B., Jr., 4, 101, 156, 157-73, 174
 on academic disciplines, 169, 214
 on Christian identity, 159-63, 172-73, 194-95
 on church and world, 159-63
 on church leadership, 157-59, 163-66
 on theological study, 166-70, 201, 204, 216
Consciousness, structures of, 122-26, 133-34
Curriculum. *See* Theological curriculum

Disciplines, academic, 18-19, 151, 168-69, 206
 institutionalization of, 61, 84-86, 214-15, 218-19

Enlightenment, 12, 64, 109, 129-30, 161
"Essences," universal, 142, 144-46, 152, 194, 217, 224. *See also* Pluralism; Universalizing, misplaced
 of Christianity, 17, 22, 24
 of reason, 187-88
 of subjectivity, 130-34
Experience, 137-41, 193-94
 and God, 139, 142, 147-48
 and language, 148
 women's, 137

Faculties, professionalization of, 84-86
Faith. *See Theologia:* and faith
Fallon, Daniel, 18
Farley, Edward, 4, 7, 100, 141, 143, 152, 159, 219. *See also Theologia*
 on academic disciplines, 118-19, 171, 214
 on fragmentation of theological study, 158, 223
 on structure and unity of theological study, 101-3, 111-21, 165, 167
 on *theologia*, 101-34, 142, 145, 200, 201, 204
 on *Wissenschaft*, 16, 101-2, 115-16, 216
Feminism. *See* Mud Flower Collective

God:
 and experience, 139, 142, 147-48
 and justice, 143
 Niebuhr on, 71-74
 as object of *Wissenschaft*, 77-78, 81-82
Good, idea of the, 8-9
Gregory the Great, 75
Guilds, scholarly. *See* Disciplines, academic
Gustafson, James M., 64-71, 79-81, 83-84, 87, 90

Habitus, concept of:
 Farley on, 103-5, 115, 121-34, 201
 Wood on, 201-2, 213, 215-16
Harper, William Rainey, 51-54, 81, 90
Harrison, Beverly W., 135
Hermeneutics:
 classical liberal, 185-86
 Farley's five modes of, 111-21
 of suspicion, 42
Heyward, Carter, 135

Hough, Joseph C., Jr., 4, 101, 156, 157-73, 174
  on academic disciplines, 169, 214
  on Christian identity, 159-63, 172-73, 194-95
  on church and world, 159-63
  on church leadership, 157-59, 163-66
  on theological study, 166-70, 201, 204, 216
Human nature, conception of, 150, 152, 188, 217, 228. *See also* Reason, conception of
  in "Athens" model, 26, 44-47
  in "Berlin" model, 26-27
  classical versus modern, 122-23, 126-28
  as social, 45-47, 223-24
Humboldt, Wilhelm von, 12-13, 18, 23, 25-26, 69

Ideology, 47, 53
  and critical inquiry, 61-62, 64, 89, 148-49, 171, 210
  and ministerial authority, 82-83
  and social location of learning, 218
Isasi-Diaz, Ada Maria, 135

Jaeger, Werner, 7, 9
Johnson, Bess B., 135
Justice, 138-41, 143-44, 150. *See also* Social location of learning
  Stackhouse on, 180-82

Kelly, Robert L., 54-64, 65, 72, 81

Language, religious, 147-48
Leavitt, Harold J., 164

May, Mark A., 54
Ministry. *See* Church leadership

Mud Flower Collective, 2, 4, 100, 135-53, 155
  on misplaced universalizing, 137-38, 140, 209-10
  on pluralism, 137, 144-47
  on theological study and experience, 138-41
  on theological study as oriented toward justice, 143-44, 146

Newman, John Henry, 30-47, 118
  concept of "gentleman," 35, 43
  on goal of university, 32-39
  "innocent theorizing" of, 47, 119, 224
  on rationality, 33, 38, 43-44, 109, 133, 142, 145
  on unity of truth, 39-41
  view of human nature, 44-47
Niebuhr, H. Richard, 71-89, 101, 143, 160
  on internal movement of theological study, 86-89, 178
  on minister as pastoral director, 74-76
  on the purpose of the church, 72-74, 158-59
  radical monotheism of, 72-74
  in *The Advancement of Theological Education,* 64-71, 79, 83, 87, 90
  on theological school, 77-81, 171
  on unity of theological study, 78-79
Niebuhr, Reinhold, 63n.9

Origen, 11

Paideia, 6-11, 47-48, 181. *See also* "Athens" model; *Theologia*
  ahistorical character of, 109
  Christianity as, 7, 10-11, 47-48
  Mud Flower Collective version of, 141-47

Newman's version of, 32-39
public character of, 7
teacher's role in, 20, 107, 141
Paulsen, Friedrich, 26
Pellauer, Mary D., 135
Plato, 8-9
Pluralism, 95-100, 135, 221-25. *See
also* "Christian thing"; Relativism; Social location of learning
of "Christian identity," 172-73,
196
Farley on, 108, 129-31, 134
irreducibility of, 136-37, 142, 144-
47, 152, 194
and justice, 138-41, 143-44
kinds of, 98-100
and rationality, 188
Professional education:
functionalist view of, 50, 52, 57-
59, 62
Newman on, 36-37
theological study as:
in Hough and Cobb, 157-59,
163-66
in Niebuhr, 71-72, 77-78
in Schleiermacher, 15-16, 24-25,
53, 174

Reason, conception of. *See also*
Human nature, conception of;
Universalizing, misplaced
in "Athens" model, 26-27
in "Berlin" model, 26-27
in Newman, 33, 38, 43-44
in Stackhouse, 187-88, 190-91
Relativism, 175-77, 187-88
Religion, 129-30
Religious studies, 84
Richardson, Nancy D., 135

Sanneh, Lamin, 177n.8
Schleiermacher, Friedrich, 52, 53, 56,
63, 65

on professional education, 15-16,
23-25, 57, 72, 174
on structure of theological study,
17-18, 60, 184, 211
on *Wissenschaft,* 12-13, 50
Schoen, Donald, 165
Social location of learning, 42, 45-47,
108, 142-44, 146-47, 218-19.
See also Pluralism
Social sciences, 50, 52, 67
Stackhouse, Max L., 4, 101, 173-88
on apologetics, 182-84
on *praxis,* 180-82
on reason, 187-88, 190-91
on theological curriculum, 184-87
on truth, 175-80, 182-88

Teacher-student relation:
in "Athens" model, 20-21, 32-39
in "Berlin" model, 23, 68-71
Theologia (Farley). *See also* "Athens"
model; Paideia
ahistorical character of, 128-34,
145, 159
and clergy education, 116-17, 120-
21
as dialectical, 105-6, 121-28
and faith, 103, 110-11
as *habitus,* 103-5, 115, 121-28,
130-31, 201
inner movement of, 109-19, 219
and pluralism, 108
as wisdom, 102, 104, 191
Theological curriculum, 69, 169-70,
222. *See also* Disciplines, academic
contextual nature of, 118, 144
fragmentation of, 59-61, 67
Schleiermacher's threefold, 17-18,
184
unified by common interest, 213
Theological education:
goal of, 48, 67, 222-25
apologetics as, 174, 177, 184

church leadership as, 72-76, 82,
  157
justice as, 143, 146
theological inquiry as, 200, 213
wisdom as, 120, 128
unity of, 59-61, 68, 78-79, 97-98
  church leadership as basis for,
    157, 170
  essentialist views of, 101-2, 120,
    128, 151-52, 176-77, 190
  pluralist views of, 142, 146, 206-
    12
  and professionalization, 83-86
Theological schools, 96-97, 106-7
and church, 76-77, 81, 171
as professional schools, 54-64, 71-
  72, 157
resources of, 66-67
standards of, 55-56, 66, 91-93
Theology, pictures of:
as activity of inquiry, 201-13
as personal wisdom, 19-22, 109-
  15, 191-94
as reflection on experience, 138-41,
  193-94
as reflective practice, 165-66, 171-
  72, 194-96
as theory-to-application, 22-23, 80,
  86-89, 180-82, 187, 189-91
Truth. *See also* Reason, conception of;
  Relativism
Newman on unity of, 39-41

and philosophical theology, 205
Stackhouse on, 175-80, 182-88

Universalizing, misplaced, 137-38,
  140, 209-10
Universals, 144, 149-50, 152
University:
Newman on purpose of, 32-39
research and, 12-14, 29-30, 35-37
theology in, 14-18, 39-41
University of Berlin, 12, 16, 18, 56, 63
University of Chicago, 51, 53

Williams, Daniel Day, 64-71, 79-81,
  83-84, 87, 90
Wissenschaft, 12-19, 24, 26
God as object of, 77-78, 81-82
and *habitus,* 124-28, 215-16
as ideology critique, 90-91, 149,
  227
and paideia, 102, 104-5, 115, 118,
  122
and professionalism, 50, 59-63, 65,
  157, 170-71
and teaching, 23, 67, 68-70
Wood, Charles, 4, 101, 200-220
on concepts as capacities, 215-16
on theology as inquiry, 200-212
on vision and discernment, 203,
  208-11